PACKAGE
PROMOTE
SCALE

GROW YOUR BUSINESS
REVENUE
AND
IMPACT
WITHOUT THE STRESS AND OVERWHELM

ROB NAGY & JODIE WILLMER
...your consulting business guides!

"*Package Promote Scale is a transformative guide for consultants who want to grow their business while maintaining balance. Rob Nagy and Jodie Willmer have created an actionable framework that simplifies the complexities of consulting into nine clear steps, helping you package your services, promote your expertise, and scale your impact. The real-world case studies and practical insights provide invaluable tools for consultants looking to elevate their practice. This book is not just theory, it's a proven roadmap for success. Whether you're just starting or looking to refine your approach, this is a must-read for all consultants.*"

– Andrew Griffiths, International Bestselling Business Author, Global Speaker

"*Happy Changemakers have transformed my wellness business with their Package Promote Scale Framework. They helped me package my services into the Wellness Business HUB, market effectively and scale effortlessly.*

I'm now working smarter, not harder and have significantly increased my impact and my income, resulting in a much better work-life balance."

– Christine Boucher, CEO, Wellness Worx

"*Package Promote Scale is a game-changer for independent consultants seeking growth without sacrificing their well-being. With the PPS framework, practical tips, and real-world case studies, this book empowers consultants to achieve success while maintaining a healthy work-life balance, aligning with their values and vision for impact.*"

– Jacqui Blanch, Founder, DigiHearth

"Robert and Jodie offer a practical and realistic approach in their work. They share their expertise with the world in a way that's both insightful and accessible, making it easy for consultants to streamline their services and scale their businesses. Their PPS framework is a game-changer!"

– Martin J Cowling, Founder, *"Change, Leadership, Impact."*

"Do yourself a favour and read this book. It's a valuable resource that will save you the time and effort of figuring out how to get your work into the world. If you are a consultant with big ideas and an appetite for big impact, if you're starting out or doing a revamp, this book is a must-read. It's full of valuable advice, not your ordinary framework but authentic and practical. This is your go-to resource for making the impact you intend and will help you literally package, promote and scale your work."

– Tathra Street, Leadership Futurist

"I am a massive fan of the individual consultants and what they can do for Profit and For Purpose businesses. What Jodie and Rob has been able to achieve with this book is to really hone down the core concepts needed to be a success. And don't you owe that to your clients?"

– Scott Trevethan, Founder & CEO, Financial Fanatics

"Love the PPS framework! This book is a great guide and helped me to package my services more effectively. Jodie and Rob share practical guidance that really works. It's been so useful when speaking with new clients about my offerings and helped me stay focused on a business and life balance that works for me."

– Leanne Hart, Founder, Hart2heart Wellbeing

"Launching a consulting business in my 60s was tougher than expected. Jodie and Rob's guidance was a lifeline. Their framework helped me clarify my value and find ideal clients. Bundling my services was a revelation – suddenly, I had a thriving business and a flexible schedule. It felt like a whole new chapter unfolding."

– Janis McKenna, Founder and Managing Director,
Elm Consulting Australia

"As a consultant, I'm always looking for ways to make simple changes to get big results. This book helped me do exactly that. After following this simple, yet effective process, I've now completely reshaped the way that I structure and talk about my services, which my clients love! Highly recommend."

– Andrew Wilson, Director | Business Planning Specialist,
Horizon Business Plans

"Every time I have turned to Jodie for mentoring over the last few years, I have been blown away by her knowledge and wisdom. I'm yet to find a business challenge she hasn't been able to talk me through. She has seen me through strategic transitions and challenges and has felt like a guardian angel who always has my back. Thanks Jodie."

– Renée Hasseldine, Founder, Think RAPT

"I thought I had all the elements I needed for my business – but I was all over the place with inefficiencies, missed opportunities and revenue, until I read this book. Following the framework and great advice I worked through changes at my own pace and capacity, achieving the focus and enhancements needed in my business."

– Melissa Tandy, Managing Director, Strategic Shift Consulting

"I had the privilege to beta test the Package Promote Scale 2-day Intensive program. It was like hitting the business accelerator, giving my venture the ultimate boost. Jodie and Rob, the brilliant minds behind the program, flipped the script on my business ambitions, supercharged my confidence and boosted my self-awareness - recognising my role as the guide rather than the hero. Their practical framework unlocked new possibilities, equipping me with the tools to confidently build my business. Looking for business growth? This book is your launchpad."

**– Fi Forsyth, Business Optimisation Specialist,
The Cure Coaching & Consulting**

Changemaker
associates

First published in 2025 by Changemaker Associates Pty Ltd
PO Box 275 Paynesville VIC Australia

© Robert Nagy and Jodie Willmer 2025
The moral rights of the authors have been asserted.

ISBN: 978-1-7636338-2-7

Title: Package Promote Scale
Subtitle: Grow your business revenue and impact, without the stress and overwhelm
Authors: Robert Nagy, Jodie Willmer
Editors: Denise Raven and Phaedra Pym
Cover Design: Robert Nagy

Disclaimer:

The information in this book is for general informational purposes only and is accurate as of the publication date. It does not constitute legal, financial, accounting, tax, or professional advice. No express or implied warranties are made regarding the content's accuracy, completeness, or currency.

Readers should seek independent professional advice tailored to their circumstances before making decisions based on this information. The author and publisher are not liable for any losses or damages arising from the use of this book.

Results from applying the strategies in this book may vary. Past success does not guarantee future results. References to third-party tools or services do not constitute endorsements. Readers are responsible for evaluating the suitability of any such resources.

This book is intended for independent consultants running small-scale businesses in Australia. Laws and regulations may differ elsewhere. Those accessing this book from other jurisdictions should ensure compliance with local laws.

By using this book, you acknowledge and accept this disclaimer. If you do not agree, please refrain from using the book.

Contents

To our mothers who are no longer with us but whose eternal love and belief in us continue to guide our steps. We love you and miss you dearly. Your memory is our everlasting inspiration.

Foreword

I've long admired Jodie and Rob's commitment to work-life balance. Many teach it, even preach it, but few truly practice it. Jodie and Rob not only model it in their lives but also help others achieve it. Through *Package Promote Scale*, they kindly gift us a valuable approach to not only grow our business revenue and impact as independent consultants, but to also rediscover why we started our businesses in the first place. With their gentle guidance and support, we can learn to fall back in love with our business again.

As someone who has had the privilege of working alongside and learning from Jodie Willmer for more than 20 years, I've witnessed firsthand the impact of the Package Promote Scale Framework on many service-based businesses. When I find myself not valuing my time or I'm problem-solving within my own business, it is Jodie's voice that guides me.

Throughout my 25 years in leadership roles across various businesses and agencies, I've encountered a common thread among independent consultants: burnout. Having been there myself, I know all too well how our desire to make an impact can be so consuming that it inadvertently depletes us.

Compounding this issue is a long-perpetuated belief that we must create beautiful, bespoke proposals for services that all too often fall outside the sweet spot where our passion, purpose and profit align. This misguided notion adds to our burden and becomes the enemy of balance.

This is where the principles covered in *Package Promote Scale* become a lifesaver.

Through Benefolk, a national professional services intermediary I founded, I've seen Jodie and Rob support the transformation of many business owners. They help restructure businesses, set boundaries, elevate prices, value time and increase productivity and joy.

The road to reducing burnout isn't doing more of what we're already doing. That's the trap many of us fall into. It takes an overhaul of your model, method and mindset, which Jodie and Rob's approach facilitates.

They also bust myths, especially for service-based businesses often caught in the mindset that services always need to be bespoke. Some of the world's best service businesses are package-focused, thinking like a product while solving like a service. And contrary to popular belief, packaged services can still be premium, just like a luxury holiday package that offers a high-end experience.

As a self-made billionaire once taught me, 'Make it easy for the customer to buy from you.' Too many options will only serve to confuse people, and they won't buy. In this book, Jodie and Rob offer a practical framework to help businesses simplify their offerings, making it easier for clients to choose.

Finally, for those who started their business to make a bigger impact in the world, your sense of urgency to scale may be even greater. Rest assured, you are not alone. Jodie and Rob are here as partners to help you create that lasting impact and legacy.

So, congratulations on taking the next big step in elevating your consulting business and enriching your life.

I wish you wellness, prosperity and joy as you grow your business.

Julia Keady
CEO/Founder, benefolk.org

Preface

Our journey to this point has been far from straightforward. A few years ago, we were struggling in the consulting industry, unsure of how to move forward. We were good at what we did but didn't know how to run a successful business that could support the life we wanted. We worked hard, taking on many projects and saying yes to every opportunity. However, despite our efforts, our bank account and stress levels told a different story.

Then something shifted. A stark realisation hit us: our business wasn't just about scraping a living; it was about living the life we had always dreamed of. This was our turning point. Armed with a whiteboard and a lot of grit, we charted the kind of business and life we truly wanted. After three gruelling yet rewarding years of reorientation and focus, we now live in a peaceful country town, successfully running our business while also helping our community recover from catastrophic fires and a global pandemic.

We wrote this book to guide you, the small business owner and consultant, away from the path of overwhelm and towards the life you envisioned when you started your business. It addresses two significant issues: revenue generation and stress management. With over 20 years of experience and the wisdom gathered from mentoring over 400 business owners, we are thrilled to present to you a system that works.

What sets this book apart? The answer lies in its framework which we've fine-tuned through years of practical application and mentorship. It focuses on action, not fluff. It's about working smarter, not harder, and flipping the narrative from 'doing more' to 'earning more while living better'. It guides you back from the brink of burnout to a balanced life where stress is a memory, not a daily routine.

If you find yourself overwhelmed with bespoke projects and see your pipeline of opportunities drying up or feel 'icky' about sales and stressed about the revenue, then this book is your lifeline. From understanding how to package your services to learning about the power of consistent promotion and how to scale your business sustainably, every step addresses common challenges faced by consultants and service providers.

We recommend reading this book sequentially. First, skim through it to grasp the overall flow, and then drill down into areas that require immediate attention in your business. Each section builds upon the previous one, leading you to a comprehensive solution.

The approach taken in the book isn't theoretical; it's derived from the school of hard knocks and has been road-tested by hundreds of consultants, including ourselves. We have used real-world examples, templates and our collective expertise, gathered over two decades.

This book provides you with a framework based on our experience and mentorship; the rest is up to you. View it as an investment in yourself and your future. Engage with it, challenge it and apply it, and watch your consulting business transform.

For more resources, visit our website, and for any queries or feedback, feel free to reach out.

Here's to packaging, promoting and scaling your way to a life and business that you love.

Rob Nagy and **Jodie Willmer**

www.packagepromotescale.com

Acknowledgements

Writing this book has been a challenging yet deeply rewarding endeavour, one that we could not have completed without the help, support, and inspiration from countless individuals. First and foremost, we want to thank our families, whose unwavering love and patience enabled us to focus on this important project. Your support is the foundation upon which we build all our successes.

We would also like to acknowledge Andrew Griffiths and Michael Hanrahan for their early feedback, guidance, and support. Your input was instrumental in shaping the direction of this work.

A special thanks to our friends in business and our mentors. Your insights, critiques and encouragement have been invaluable. We are particularly grateful to those who generously shared their case studies and testimonials for this book. You've not only enriched the content but also inspired countless readers who will follow in your footsteps.

We are grateful for the valuable feedback received from our early readers, notably Tathra Street, whose perspectives helped refine our message.

To our talented and wonderful team of editors, designers and marketing staff, your hard work and dedication have turned our vision into a reality. Your professionalism and talents have exceeded all expectations, and we couldn't be prouder of the result.

We want to acknowledge the numerous authors, thought leaders and industry experts whose work has influenced us. Your groundbreaking ideas and strategies have shaped our thinking and practices in the consulting world, and this book is a testament to that accumulated wisdom.

A heartfelt thanks to our community of consultants. Interacting with you, understanding your challenges and celebrating your successes have given us a deeper understanding of the impact we wish to create. You are the reason we wrote this book, and we are committed to your growth and success.

A huge shout out to you, our readers. Your interest and engagement make all our efforts worthwhile. We wrote this book to help you transform your consultancy practice, and it is your willingness to take action that will determine its ultimate success.

Finally, we are excited about the future and look forward to crossing paths in new ways as we all continue to *Package Promote Scale* our visions into reality.

Introduction

Are you a consultant who feels buried under endless client work, administrative tasks and a never-ending quest for new business? Do you find yourself lying awake at night, contemplating how to scale your consulting business without losing yourself in the process? If you nodded in agreement, then you've picked up the right book.

Welcome to *Package Promote Scale—Grow your business revenue and impact, without the stress and overwhelm.* This isn't just another business book that showers you with platitudes and leaves you to figure out the rest. This is a step-by-step guide, born from the trenches of the consulting industry, that will walk you through the actionable and measurable phases of our Package Promote Scale Framework.

Ahead of you is a clear road map with three phases, each broken down into three practical steps. Just nine steps to build a more streamlined, profitable and scalable consulting business. This framework isn't theory; it's a field-tested methodology that we have used to not only scale our own consulting business but have also shared with countless other consultants to achieve similar results.

Why this book, you ask? Because there's an ocean of information out there but only a drop of wisdom that truly works. If you're tired of the hustle, the anxiety and the operational chaos that accompanies the life of a consultant, then it's time to let go of the things that are weighing you down and move forward.

***

WHAT YOU WILL GAIN FROM THIS BOOK

Now that you know why you're here, let's talk about what you'll walk away with after reading this book:

- **Clarity And Efficiency Through Packaging**

  Most consultants get bogged down in customisation. In the first phase of our framework, Package, you'll learn how to simplify your offerings into scalable solutions. You will get tools and strategies to identify your core services, test them in the market and refine them based on feedback.

- **Effective Promotion Without The Frustration**

  Gone are the days when a consultant could rely solely on word-of-mouth referrals. The Promote phase will equip you with the simple yet effective approach for a solid marketing strategy, launching your offerings and managing an active pipeline.

- **Scalability Without Chaos**

  The key to scaling a consulting business is to do it without overwhelming yourself and your team. In the Scale phase, you'll discover how to put systems in place, build a capable team and optimise your business for continuous growth.

- **Mindset Shifts**

  Beyond the practical steps and tools, this book will challenge you to shift your mindset. To truly scale, you'll need to think differently about your role, your time and your value. We consider these mindset shifts in each phase of our framework.

By the end of this book, you won't just have theoretical knowledge; you'll have a game plan you can begin implementing immediately. In a world where time is your most precious resource, we aim to make every second you invest in this book well worth it.

***

HOW THIS BOOK IS STRUCTURED

Understanding the layout and flow of this book will help you get the most out of it.

The Framework: *Package Promote Scale*

The book is divided into three main sections, with each one corresponding to a phase in the Package Promote Scale Framework. Within each section you'll discover three steps dedicated to a specific aspect of that phase.

Here's the breakdown:

Phase 1: Package

- *Step 1: Design* – Streamline your services for efficiency.
- *Step 2: Test* – Validate your offerings in the real world.
- *Step 3: Refine* – Evolve based on genuine feedback.

Phase 2: Promote

- *Step 4: Attract* – Draw in potential clients through effective positioning.
- *Step 5: Connect* – Build and nurture client relationships.
- *Step 6: Nurture* – Maintain and deepen client engagement.

Phase 3: Scale

- *Step 7: Integrate* – Optimise your business operations.
- *Step 8: Amplify* – Build a capable, efficient team.
- *Step 9: Optimise* – Continuously improve for lasting success.

Case Studies And Examples

Integrated into each step are case studies and examples from other consulting businesses that have successfully implemented the strategies we discuss. These practical insights aim to provide a practical lens through which you can see the concepts in action.

Action Steps And Resources

Each step closes with a set of practical action steps, and our website at www.packagepromotescale.com will contain valuable checklists, templates and exercises to help turn theory into practice.

***

PRACTICAL WAYS TO ENGAGE WITH THIS BOOK

Now that you know what to expect from the pages that follow, let's explore how to make the most out of this book. The Package Promote Scale Framework is designed to be both versatile and practical, but its efficacy depends on how actively you engage with the material. Here are a few pointers to help you get the most out of this book.

- **Start With A Self-Assessment**

  Before leaping into the first step, take some time to assess the current state of your consulting business. Identify which phase – Package, Promote or Scale – requires your most immediate attention. Then either read it in order for a complete model or jump to steps that address your immediate needs.

- **Take Notes And Highlights**

  As you read through each step, make a habit of taking notes and highlighting key points that resonate with you. Jot down how these points could apply to your specific situation. These annotations will serve as quick references and reminders for action items.

- **Complete The Action Steps**

  Don't skip over these! The action steps are there to turn abstract theory into tangible practice. The more you put into them, the more you'll get out of the entire framework.

- **Engage With Case Studies**

  The case studies within each step offer a valuable real-world context to the strategies discussed. Read them carefully and consider how the examples relate to your own business challenges and goals.

- **Keep A Progress Journal**

  Create a dedicated journal or digital document where you can track your progress through each phase and step. Write down challenges, successes and lessons learned. This journal will not only keep you accountable but also offer insights into your growth and areas for improvement.

- **Revisit And Revise**

  The Package Promote Scale Framework isn't something you do once and forget. It's a process of continuous improvement. After each change, review the results and decide what to improve next.

- **Connect And Share**

  Feel free to connect with us and other readers on social media platforms where we regularly share additional tips, updates and success stories. It's more rewarding when you engage with a community that offers support, feedback, and fresh perspectives.

- **Measure Your Success**

  What gets measured gets managed. Regularly evaluate your performance metrics to ensure you're moving in the right direction. Consider setting up a dashboard that tracks each key performance indicator (KPI) relevant to each phase of the framework.

***

These practical guidelines are here to help you fully engage with this book, making it a meaningful resource that enhances your consulting business while keeping things manageable and stress-free.

GROWING A CONSULTING BUSINESS YOU LOVE

Mastering the art of consultancy isn't merely about becoming better at what you do. It's about becoming better at how you do it. The Package Promote Scale Framework isn't just a set of instructions but our proven approach aimed at sustained growth and quality of life. Your consulting business needs to serve you as much as you serve your clients, and this book is your guide to making that a reality.

In the following sections, you'll find a wealth of information, tactics and strategies, each tailored to guide you through the three phases and nine steps that we have meticulously developed.

This book is more than a one-time read; it's as a resource to revisit. As the business landscape shifts, technology progresses, and client needs change, adaptability is your key to thriving. You can always return to these pages whenever you need a refresher, new ideas, or support with challenges.

Thank you for trusting us to be a part of your growth. We can't wait to see where the Package Promote Scale Framework takes you.

The Problem We're Solving

THE CURRENT STATE OF CONSULTING

Consulting is transforming rapidly as the need for specialised skills grows. This is great news for consultants, but it also comes with challenges like fierce competition, quickly changing markets, and clients who expect more.

THE CHALLENGES YOU FACE

- **Competition**

  You're not only competing against traditional consulting firms. There are freelancers, niche consulting companies and even AI-powered solutions all vying for the same projects and clients.

- **Skill Diversification**

  You're expected to wear multiple hats – project manager, expert adviser, marketer and more. While being a multiskilled asset is valuable, it's easy to get overwhelmed.

- **Work-Life Balance**

  In an industry where client expectations are high, you often end up sacrificing personal time to keep up. This can lead to burnout, which may impact the quality of your work and, ultimately, your reputation.

- **Client Expectations**

  With more information at their fingertips, clients now expect you to offer more than just advice. They want results they can measure and act on.

- **Revenue Inconsistency**

  Many consultants face the feast-or-famine cycle, a stressful oscillation between having either too much or not enough work.

***

THE NEED FOR A GUIDING FRAMEWORK

If you're like most consultants, you're looking for ways to break through these challenges and uncertainties to achieve consistent success. You want to be seen as the go-to expert in your field, attract and retain quality clients, generate consistent revenue and still have time for a fulfilling personal life. To do that, you need more than just a patchwork of tactics and tips; you need a comprehensive, actionable framework.

WHAT SETS THIS BOOK APART

- **A Proven Framework**

  It's not about isolated tactics. It's a tried-and-true, step-by-step approach that you can tailor to suit the specific needs of your consulting business.

- **Actionable Steps**

  Each phase and step is accompanied by actionable recommendations, templates and real-world examples.

- **Addresses the Whole Picture**

  This book doesn't just focus on one aspect of consulting, such as marketing or service delivery. It offers a holistic view that ties together all the elements essential for long-term success.

- **Empowers You**

  Instead of just giving you a fish, we teach you how to fish. The aim is to empower you with the tools and mindset to make the best decisions for your own circumstances.

WHAT YOU WILL ACHIEVE

- **Clarity**

  Gain a clear understanding of where your consulting business stands, where it could go and how to get there.

- **Direction**

  The framework serves as your guide, helping you manage the complexities of running a consulting business.

- **Efficiency**

  Implement best practices that optimise your time and resources so you can focus on what really matters.

- **Sustainability**

  Learn how to build a business that's not only profitable in the short term but also sustainable in the long run.

***

This book is your resource for building a consulting business that thrives. With a clear framework, actionable steps, and a holistic approach, you'll be equipped to achieve clarity, direction, efficiency, and sustainability in your work. It's about empowering you to make informed decisions and create lasting success in your business.

Understanding the Package Promote Scale Framework

In this section, we'll unravel the core principles of the framework we've designed to elevate your consulting business to new heights, sustainably and efficiently.

FRAMEWORK OVERVIEW

The consulting industry has its challenges, but it also offers great opportunities. Whether you're well-established or just starting out, moving from surviving to thriving requires more than just a set of skills. It takes a well-structured approach. This is where the Package Promote Scale Framework comes into play, providing you with a road map for success in your consulting business.

The Core Philosophy

The essence of this framework lies in its simplicity. It's designed to guide you through the critical phases of running a successful consulting business, each representing a pillar that supports the edifice of your enterprise.

The framework is structured around three main phases:

- **Phase 1: Package**
- **Phase 2: Promote**
- **Phase 3: Scale**

These phases are not merely stand-alone modules; they are interlinked components of a cohesive strategy. They inform and enhance one another, creating a harmonious cycle that allows for growth, efficiency and overall business stability.

***

The Three Phases Explained

Phase 1: Package

The first phase is about laying a strong foundation for your business. It focuses on your core offerings, helping you define them clearly and package them effectively. You're not trying to be everything to everyone. Instead, you are concentrating on what you do best, creating targeted service packages that resonate with your ideal client's needs.

Phase 2: Promote

Once your offerings are well-packaged and your value proposition is crystal clear, the next step is to make sure that the right people know about it. The Promote phase is all about getting your services in front of your target audience through effective marketing strategies. This is not about casting a wide net but about targeted marketing using specific channels and tactics to reach potential clients who align with your business values and offerings.

Phase 3: Scale

Finally, having established your core offerings and made them known to your ideal clientele, the Scale phase focuses on growing your business while maintaining or improving quality. This involves systematising your operations and building a team that can help you manage an increased workload, allowing you to take on more clients or bigger projects without diluting your service quality.

A 9-Step Approach

The framework is structured around three key phases, with each phase consisting of three steps, making it a nine-step approach to transforming your business. These steps ensure that you're actively applying the strategies for the best possible results.

***

Refer to the diagram on the following page for a visual representation of how these phases and steps are interconnected, providing a clear path to success in your consulting business.

To download a high-quality version of the framework please visit: www.packagepromotescale.com/framework

Package

1. Design

Create a solution to address a specific need or problem...

2. Test

Introduce your solution to a handful of your contacts...

3. Refine

Make adjustments to your solution based on their input...

Promote

4. Attract

Position yourself as someone with the solution people are looking for...

5. Connect

Utilise your existing relationships to reach potential clients...

6. Nurture

Build and maintain strong relationships by consistently offering value...

Scale

7. Integrate

Use systems and processes to streamline your workflow...

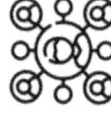

8. Amplify

Grow your capability and capacity with the right team...

9. Optimise

Review and tweak your business practices for the best results...

WHY WE NEED A FRAMEWORK

So, why do we even need a framework when countless businesses run without ever adopting one? If, like most business owners, you operate by tapping into your knowledge, experience, and intuition, there are still a few good reasons for introducing a framework into the way you run your business:

- **Managing Complexity**

  Consulting can be complicated. You're working with people and building relationships, rather than dealing with products. Each client project comes with its own challenges. A framework helps you manage this complexity and stay on track.

- **Staying Focused**

  Working without a framework is like moving without direction. You might get somewhere, but it may not be where you want to go. A framework helps you plan ahead, spot challenges and opportunities, and make smarter decisions that align with your goals.

- **Accountability And Performance Metrics**

  In the absence of a system, evaluating your business performance becomes a nebulous endeavour. A framework introduces KPIs specific to each phase, making it easier to track your progress and hold yourself accountable. It allows you to diagnose bottlenecks, celebrate wins and generally understand how well you're doing in quantifiable terms.

- **Long-Term Resilience**

  While ad hoc solutions might offer short-term gains, they're often unsustainable in the long run. A framework like Package Promote Scale is engineered for durability. It is designed to adapt and grow with your business, providing a long-term solution that prepares you for market volatility and keeps you ahead of the competition.

- **Cohesive Team Dynamics**

  In running a business with multiple people involved, including staff, sub-contractors, or others, having a standardised framework ensures that everyone is on the same page. It eliminates ambiguity and promotes a unified approach to tackling challenges. In simpler terms, it turns a group of individuals into a well-coordinated team.

  ***

In the following chapters, we'll unpack the three phases and nine steps of the Package Promote Scale Framework. Each phase builds on the last, guiding you through a structured approach to clarify your offer, attract aligned opportunities, and scale your consulting business with confidence. Whether you're working solo or leading a small team, this framework provides the clarity, structure, and momentum you need to grow sustainably.

Phase 1: Package

Your objective in the first phase of the Package Promote Scale Framework is to streamline your service offerings into a limited set of packages. These packages should be ready to go yet flexible enough to tailor to the specific needs of your most aligned clients. This approach counters the time-consuming challenge of creating bespoke solutions for every new client who comes to you with a unique requirement. By the end of this phase, you'll have specialised packages that save you time and position you as the go-to person in your field for the specific types of problems you solve and the results you deliver.

Step 1 – Design

Imagine walking into a bustling restaurant. You hear the soft hum of conversations and the delicate chime of silverware, as the inviting aroma of delicious food wafts through the air. As you scan the menu, you're instantly drawn to the chef's special. It sounds mouthwatering. This is clearly a dish crafted from years of experience, using the freshest ingredients and designed to appeal to a broad range of tastes. Now, imagine if every customer asked the chef to make a special dish just for them instead of ordering from the menu. How long would service take? How consistent would the quality be? And can you imagine the stress the kitchen would be under? It's almost laughable to think of a restaurant operating that way, isn't it? Yet in many ways, this mirrors the world of bespoke work versus packaging in consulting.

Just like that chef has a specialty dish, as consultants, we have our own expertise which we can package into a targeted offering that can cater to a significant segment of our clientele. Packaging our services enables us to focus on what we do best, deliver consistent results, and streamline our processes, all while ensuring our clients get the top-notch service they expect. In contrast, bespoke work, although tailored to individual clients, can often become cumbersome and unpredictable and is not always cost-effective.

So, what can you package? Well, think about what you're truly passionate about. What drives you? Where do you see yourself making the most impact? Immerse yourself in self-examination, challenge any negative self-perceptions that might be limiting you and align your emotions with your business objectives. Your confidence in your offering will establish trust and resonate with your potential clients.

Start simple. Just like you wouldn't redesign an entire restaurant menu overnight, you don't need to create all your packages at once. Begin with just one package. The main idea here is to simplify, not complicate. Your package becomes something tangible, an offering that you can proudly present to potential clients as well as your existing network. Think of it as your promise to the market. It's not only about what you're offering but also how you present it. Crafting a message that connects emotionally, using stories and genuine communication, can make all the difference.

To create a compelling service package, focus on several key elements. First, demonstrate a proven track record of delivering successful outcomes in related areas. Next, identify a genuine market need for your package and clearly define your target clientele. Finally, articulate the unique value proposition of your offering. These factors will help ensure your service package resonates with potential clients and stands out in the market.

Importantly, this package must be something you can deliver successfully. It's about building a reputation, about showing you can consistently deliver on your promises. Keep in mind that no two clients are identical. So, while your package forms the bulk of your service, be ready to tailor about 20 per cent of it to suit the needs of each client.

Lastly, it is essential to differentiate yourself in the market. While there's value in offering a range of services, not every dish in a restaurant is for everyone. Trying to do everything or just piling on more and more packages isn't the way to go.

Designing a valuable service package is like crafting a beautiful dish. It's a testament to your expertise and passion. It means understanding your strengths, identifying your ideal clients, addressing their pain points and offering a solution that not only makes business sense but also resonates on a personal level.

Keep the chef's special in mind while we explore the intricacies of service package design. It is not solely the ingredients that make it great but also the love, care, and expertise that goes into crafting it. And just like that dish, your service package, rooted in authenticity, understanding and passion, has the potential to become a favourite among your clientele.

***

TAPPING INTO WHAT YOU LOVE DOING MOST AND YOUR 'BIG WHY'

When it comes to the services we offer, there's profound truth in the saying 'Do what you love, and you'll never work a day in your life.' For consultants, the real magic unfolds when aligning our professional offerings with what sets our hearts on fire.

Think back to when you started your business. There were probably specific aspects that drew you in, certain tasks or projects that made your heart race a little faster and moments when you felt like you were making a real difference. These are the things you genuinely love doing. It might be the satisfaction of solving a complex problem, the joy of connecting with a client or the thrill of seeing a project come to fruition.

Imagine aligning your work with these passions. Your days would not only become more enjoyable, but your energy, enthusiasm, and genuine love for the job would shine through in everything you do. Clients can sense this. They're naturally drawn to those who are authentic and passionate about their work.

Take a moment to reflect. Beyond the daily tasks and client interactions lies something even more profound: your big why. *Why* did you choose *this* business? *Why* do you wake up every morning ready to face the challenges of the day? Your big why does not only involve revenue or market standing; it's the deeper, emotional reason behind your choices.

However, you need to go beyond the act of doing what you love and think about the people you work with. Let's face it, no matter how much you enjoy the work itself, if you don't connect with your clients, it can quickly become draining. It's important that you genuinely enjoy working with the types of people you aim to attract. These are the people you'll be spending a lot of time with, collaborating, brainstorming and sharing both challenges and victories.

- Does your client appreciate your expertise and value your input?
- Do they respect your boundaries?
- Is the communication smooth and fulfilling?

Answering these questions allows you to gauge whether a client aligns with your passion and ethos.

What about when the project demands something beyond your expertise? You might be the head chef in the kitchen but sometimes you need a sous-chef or two to help bring the dish to perfection. This could be a team member or a subcontractor. Keep in mind that if you decide to offer a package that requires skills outside your wheelhouse, it's crucial to have a reliable team that resonates with your values and goals. After all, the outcome of the project isn't just a reflection of your work but also of those you partner with.

Perhaps what you love most about a career in consulting is the freedom and flexibility it offers, allowing you to spend more time with your family. Maybe it's the thrill of making a genuine difference in your clients' lives or it could be the legacy you want to leave behind. Your big why is the driving force that keeps you going, even on tough days. It's your inner North Star, guiding you through decisions, challenges and successes.

When you tap into your big why, your perspective shifts. You begin to see your business as more than just a means to an end. Instead, it becomes the vehicle enabling you to achieve your dreams. And it isn't only about your personal aspirations either. Think about the ripple effect of your success: the impact on those closest to you, the community and even society at large.

Aligning your work with your passions and deeper purpose (your 'big why') is crucial for success and fulfillment. This alignment doesn't just build a business; it creates a life that truly reflects who you are. When you love what you do and understand its meaningful impact, you're better equipped to face challenges and find lasting satisfaction.

***

CRAFTING A PROFITABLE PACKAGE THAT YOU LOVE AND CLIENTS CAN'T RESIST

Alright, let's get on with the exciting part! Imagine you've gathered all the right ingredients: you've tapped into what you genuinely enjoy doing, you've understood your deeper why. It's time now to cook up something irresistible: crafting that perfect service package.

Starting with a blank canvas, the first step is understanding the core of what you love doing. This isn't just about the broader service you offer, but the specifics. For instance, you might excel at developing sustainable funding strategies for grassroots organisations. Alternatively, your strength could lie in creating impact measurement frameworks for environmental nonprofits. Understanding your niche allows you to offer specialised services that truly make a difference in the social sector.

Once you pinpoint this, think about the real value you bring to the table. This goes beyond your time and represents the transformation you offer to your clients. You're not only selling a few hours of your expertise; you're selling a change, a solution, an improvement.

Next, consider your ideal clients. Think about their world. What do they struggle with? What are their pain points? Your package needs to be the missing puzzle piece they've been searching for.

- What are the client's main challenges?
- What are the problems that you help them solve?
- What are their goals?
- How does your service bring them closer to these goals?

Turning our attention to financials, crafting a package involves more than simply bundling services. It's about creating a profitable structure that benefits both you and the client. To achieve this, consider the following three points:

- **Know Your Worth**

  Understand the value you bring. This goes deeper than comparing market rates and recognises the distinct advantage you offer.

- **Cost Consideration**

  Determine what it costs you to deliver. Consider everything from your time, tools, potential team members and other expenses.

- **Pricing Sweet Spot**

  Find a balance. Your price needs to reflect your value and expertise while also being fair and appealing to your ideal clients.

With the logistics out of the way, we can now focus on the heart of the package. Imagine it as a story where you're taking your client from their current situation (the challenge they face) to their desired outcome (the solution you provide). Every element of your package should serve this journey. The more streamlined and clear this path is, the easier it becomes for potential clients to see the value and jump on board.

While it's essential to have a well-defined package, flexibility is key. Remember the 20 per cent rule advised earlier? While 80 per cent of your service package needs to be structured and defined, always leave room to customise approximately 20 per cent of it. This ensures you can tailor your services to fit the needs of each client, making the package truly resonate with them.

The goal to pricing your package is to move away from displaying hourly or day rates to an inclusive all-in-one price. If you can deliver the package more quickly, you don't have to charge less. In fact, that could be a premium offering as it may solve urgent and complex problems for your clients in a shortened timeframe.

Another vital aspect is standing out. The market is bustling with talented individuals, all offering fantastic services. Your package needs to be more than just another email in your client's inbox; it must capture their attention. This isn't about being flashy, but about highlighting the distinctive qualities that make your package different and better.

Lastly, and perhaps most importantly, always be cautious. While it's tempting to create multiple packages or to toss in every service you can offer, simplicity is gold. Overloading your offerings can confuse potential clients and dilute the value of your package. Instead, focus on perfecting one package. Once you see success, you can always expand and diversify your activities.

Crafting a profitable package combines both art and science. It's about blending what you love, what you're good at and what your ideal clients need. When done well, packaging not only boosts your business, it also paves the way for fulfilling, successful client relationships.

Tailored Package Examples

Here are two examples of packages that demonstrate how combining core services with additional support can create compelling offerings.

1. Business Development Plan + Mentoring

This is an example of a package offering strategic business planning combined with actionable mentoring to propel client growth and decision-making.

Price Range	From $10K to $30K+, this package offers flexibility based on client requirements and the depth of service provided.
Duration	Ranging from 6 to 12 weeks, this package is designed to accommodate varying client needs and project complexities.
Core Offering	At the heart of this package is a robust business development plan, tailored to each client's specific business goals and market dynamics.
Added Value	To empower clients, this package includes mentoring sessions. These sessions are focused on encouraging clients to take 'imperfect action', a strategy that promotes progress over perfection and helps to overcome procrastination or indecision.
Methodology	The approach combines structured planning with hands-on mentoring, guiding clients through the execution of their business development strategies.
Outcome	Clients not only gain a strategic plan but also the confidence and practical skills to implement it effectively, ensuring ongoing business growth.

2. Strategic Plan + Project Planning and Mentoring

This comprehensive package focuses on developing strategic frameworks with added project planning and mentoring to enhance client capacity and accountability.

Price Range	This package also ranges from $10K to $30K+, allowing customisation based on the scope and scale of client projects.
Duration	Flexible between 6 to 12 weeks, this package can be adapted to the specific timeline needs of each client.
Core Offering	The package includes a comprehensive strategic plan, detailing clear steps and milestones for achieving specific business objectives.
Added Value	Adding to the strategic planning is project planning and mentoring. This component is crucial for building the client's capacity and capability in managing and executing complex projects.
Methodology	A blend of strategic oversight and practical project planning, coupled with mentoring, ensures that clients are not only planning their activities effectively but also executing them efficiently.
Outcome	Clients will enhance their capabilities and achieve improved project outcomes. The package also emphasises reporting and accountability, helping clients to track progress and make informed decisions.

Both these packages demonstrate how combining core consulting services with additional mentoring and support can create a more holistic and impactful client engagement.

Steps To Creating A Package

Creating a service package that resonates with clients involves a methodical approach. Here are some practical steps you can take:

Analyse Offerings: Strengths, Weaknesses And Opportunities

- Identify what clients appreciate about your current services.
- Recognise areas that need improvement.
- Explore unmet client needs or potential new services.

Ideate The Package: Components, Value And Differentiators

- Define the main elements of your package.
- Articulate how these elements meet client challenges.
- Identify what distinguishes your package from other available options.

Develop Your Methodology: Phases, Steps And Duration

- Outline up to three clear phases (or stages/elements/components) of your process.
- Define the specific steps in your process.
- Establish the overall timeline and duration of each phase.

Define Scope And Deliverables: Inclusions, Exclusions And Expected Results

- Clearly define what is included and what is not.
- List tangible deliverables for clients.
- Describe the expected transformation or results.

Effort And Reward: Team Composition, Roles And Pricing

- Identify the team involved in delivering the package.
- Outline different roles and their contributions.
- Determine pricing, including all costs for profitability.

Consolidate The Package Using A Structured Framework

- Employ a structured framework, like a 3-phase, 9-step model, to integrate these elements into a cohesive package.

This structured approach helps create a valuable service package that is tailored to clients, providing a comprehensive and effective solution.

SETTING YOUR CLIENTS UP FOR SUCCESS: WHY YOU NEED TO CREATE A CONTAINER OF SUPPORT

Starting with something crucial yet often overlooked, imagine you're on a team where success depends on everyone working together harmoniously. You have all the right players, skills, and enthusiasm, but without a plan or support structure in place, things are likely to go haywire quickly. This same principle applies when working with our clients. We can offer the most outstanding service, but without creating a 'container of support,' we may not achieve the desired results.

When discussing a container of support, we're referring to an environment where clients feel supported, understood, and guided throughout the entire process. It's akin to providing them with a map, ensuring they never feel lost and always know the next step.

So, why is this container so important?

Clarity is king. When clients know what to expect, the anxiety of the unknown is minimised. They know where they are, where they're headed and how they'll get there. This doesn't just mean laying out a plan but also involves regularly checking in and updating them on progress. The more informed they are, the more comfortable and involved they feel.

Then there's the trust factor. Trust extends beyond delivering on promises; trust involves showing genuine care for the client's wellbeing. Providing constant support sends a clear message: I've got your back. This creates a bond of trust, ensuring the client feels safe and confident in your guidance.

Consider the essential elements of this container:

- **Clear Communication**

  Foster effective two-way communication. Regular updates, open channels for queries and active listening are all vital.

- **Resources**

  Provide clients with the tools and information they need. This could be in the form of documents, guides or even simple FAQs. By equipping them, you empower them.

- **Availability**

  Ensure clients know when and how they can reach out. You don't have to be on call 24/7. Set boundaries but also make them feel heard and attended to.

- **Feedback Loops**

  Encourage feedback. Not only does it provide valuable insights but it also makes the client feel involved and valued.

When these elements align, clients become active participants rather than passive recipients. They're not only depending on you; they're working alongside you. This collaboration, this partnership, can be the key to unlocking true success.

While the focus is on supporting our clients, it's essential not to forget ourselves. Creating a container of support also means setting boundaries. It's about ensuring we're not stretched too thin and that our wellbeing is also prioritised. A well-supported consultant can provide even better support to their clients.

In the bigger picture, this container isn't just a strategy or a tool; it's a philosophy. It is a commitment to ensuring success is about more than just the end goal but is also about the process. It's acknowledging that while our expertise and services are crucial, the environment we create around them can be the real game changer.

Focusing on both the 'what' and the 'how' involves building a solid container of support. When our clients succeed, we succeed too.

***

SETTING REALISTIC EXPECTATIONS AND HEALTHY BOUNDARIES

Here's the thing about consulting: we're in the business of helping, guiding and providing solutions. It feels amazing when we can assist our clients in achieving their goals. As passionate as we are about what we do, striking a balance is crucial. That balance comes from setting realistic expectations and healthy boundaries.

When we set the right expectations, we're making a commitment to our clients about what we can deliver. Honestly, there's nothing more satisfying than fulfilling a promise. However, overpromising and underdelivering can lead to disappointment for both us and our clients.

Here's how to set realistic expectations:

- **Be Clear From The Start**

  Before any project kicks off, have a candid conversation about what can be achieved and in what timeframe. Don't just tell them what they want to hear; be genuine.

- **Understand Their Needs**

  This goes beyond just knowing what they want. Dive deeper. Understand the why behind their requirements. This will give you a clearer picture of what you need to prioritise.

- **Stay Informed And Updated**

  Things change and that's okay. If there are any changes or potential delays, communicate these to the client. They will appreciate being kept in the loop.

Turning to the topic of boundaries, just like in any relationship, setting boundaries in consulting fosters respect, clarity, and prevents burnout. This isn't about keeping clients at arm's length, but about creating a space where both parties feel valued and respected.

Here are ways to maintain these healthy boundaries:

- **Define Your Availability**

  Clearly communicate your working hours and stick to them. This not only helps you recharge but also teaches clients to respect your time.

- **Learn To Say No**

  It might be tempting to take on every project or request that comes your way, but overextending yourself can lead to decreased quality of work. If something doesn't align with your expertise or schedule, it's alright to decline it.

- **Stay True To Your Expertise**

  Clients come to you because of your expertise. If they suggest something you believe won't work, voice your concerns. It's your responsibility to guide them in the right direction.

What happens if, despite all this, things don't go according to plan? Well, that's okay too. It's essential to approach such situations with understanding and a problem-solving mindset. Listen to your client's concerns, acknowledge the challenges and work together to find a solution.

Setting realistic expectations and healthy boundaries isn't just a strategy; it's a way of achieving long-term success and sustainability in the consulting world. This means honouring both our clients and ourselves. Being transparent, clear, and respectful paves the way for fulfilling and successful collaborations.

Even though our commitment to our clients is unwavering, we must also commit to ourselves. And this means setting those expectations and boundaries, not as barriers but as the framework for a relationship built on trust, respect and mutual success.

PRICING YOUR PACKAGE FOR VALUE AND PROFIT

We've all been there. Staring at our notes, trying to figure out the perfect number to scribble down for our package price. Should we aim high, go low or hit somewhere in the middle? However, there's more to pricing than just picking a random number and hoping for the best. It's a thoughtful process that, when done right, can be both rewarding for you and valuable for your clients.

When we mention pricing, we are referring to more than just money. Price is a reflection of the value you bring, the expertise you offer and the results you promise. Setting the right price is a bit like finding the perfect pair of shoes. It has to fit just right. Not too tight, not too loose.

Here are some simple tips to help you step in the right direction:

- **Know Your Worth**

  As mentioned earlier, recognising your value is essential. Before setting a price, consider your expertise, the unique blend of skills and capabilities you bring and the transformative solutions you provide. Your price needs to reflect this distinct value. If you undervalue yourself, clients might too.

- **Research Is Key**

  It's always a good idea to look around and see what others in your field are charging. This doesn't mean you have to follow the herd but it gives you a ballpark figure.

- **Costs, Costs, Costs**

  When you price a package, you're not only charging for the hours you work. Consider any overheads or out-of-pocket expenses you might have. These need to be factored into your price to ensure you're actually making a profit.

- **Value Over Price**

  When setting a price, focus on the value you offer. Clients aren't just paying for your time; they're investing in solutions, results and outcomes. The more value you can provide, the more justified your price will be.

- **Room To Move**

  It's alright to have a flexible pricing model. You could consider offering different tiers of packages. This way, clients can choose a package that fits their needs and budget.

- **Review And Revise**

  The business environment is always changing and so should your prices. Regularly review your pricing structure. If you find you're swamped with work and have too little time, maybe it's a sign that you can charge more and be selective about who you choose to work with.

Equally important is communication. Discussing money can sometimes feel a bit awkward, but it's crucial to be transparent and upfront with your clients about pricing. This approach helps avoid any surprises down the track. When discussing prices, approach the conversation with confidence. Clients aren't just paying for a service; they're investing in the results you help them achieve.

You might encounter situations where clients want to negotiate or feel your prices are a bit steep. That's fine. Listen to their concerns, explain the value you offer, and, if needed, explore any flexibility in your pricing. Avoid underselling yourself. You've worked hard to get where you are, and your prices need to reflect that.

Pricing is something of an art and a science. It's about understanding your worth, recognising the value you provide and ensuring that, at the end of the day, you're compensated fairly. Your package isn't just a list of services; it's a solution to your client's problem. And solutions, my friend, are invaluable.

As you move forward with your business and packages, welcome the need for pricing them right. See it as an opportunity to not only grow your business but also reinforce the incredible value and expertise you bring to the table. So, the next time you're pondering over numbers, take a deep breath, trust in your abilities and price with confidence.

***

CONCLUSION

In this step, we explored crafting a service package that stands out and makes clients sit up and take notice. Along the way, we unravelled many ideas, some straightforward and some a bit more complex, but all essential in their own right.

We started out by tapping into what you truly love doing – your North Star – and letting it guide you in the direction you're meant to go. When you work with passion, it is less about money or accolades and more about the joy of doing something you love and making a difference in the process.

We also talked about crafting a package that's both profitable and irresistible. It's a balancing act of sorts. On one side, you have your dreams, aspirations and financial goals. On the other, you have the needs of your clients, constantly shifting and evolving. The magic happens when these two sides meet in perfect harmony, creating a package that's as rewarding for you as it is valuable for your clients.

Then, we discussed the importance of setting up our clients for success. Think of it as laying down a path for them, filled with support, guidance and all the tools they need to succeed. When clients feel supported, they're more likely to trust you, value your expertise and stick around for the long haul.

Setting realistic expectations and healthy boundaries was also explored. This is about setting out the rules of the game right from the start. When both you and your clients know what to expect, there's clarity, understanding and mutual respect.

Lastly, we explored setting the right pricing. We discovered that it's not only about putting a price tag on your services. It's about understanding your worth, gauging the value you offer and ensuring that at the end of the day, you walk away with a sense of achievement and the compensation you deserve.

A few themes ran through the sections we covered in this step:

- **Being True To Yourself**

  Whether it's choosing a niche or setting a price, always stay true to who you are and what you believe in.

- **Understanding And Valuing Clients**

  It's more than selling a service. It's about building relationships, understanding client needs and offering genuine solutions.

- **Continual Learning And Adaptation**

  The business landscape is constantly shifting. Always be open to learning and adapting to stay ahead of the curve.

- **Integrity And Authenticity**

  In everything you do, be authentic. Let your integrity shine through, making you a trusted and respected figure in your field.

- **Taking Care Of Yourself**

  While it's important to cater to the needs of your clients, never neglect yourself. A happy, contented and well-rested you can achieve so much more.

- **Effective Communication**

  Whether it's setting expectations or discussing prices, effective communication is key. It clears up any misunderstandings and paves the way for strong, lasting relationships.

- **Taking Action**

  Dreams and plans are great but it's action that truly counts. Don't be afraid to take that leap, make mistakes, learn and grow.

As we conclude this step, it's important to recognise that you have the power to create something truly special. The insights and ideas we've shared are tools in your toolkit. How you use, adapt, and make them your own is entirely up to you.

The path ahead will have its ups and downs, but with determination, passion, and a clear sense of purpose, no challenge is too big in your journey to building a successful consulting business. So as you move on to the next step, do so with hope, confidence, and the belief that the best is yet to come.

***

CASE STUDY

Meet Ellen, a talented fundraising consultant with big dreams. She wanted to boost her earnings but without the added stress and overwhelm that often came with it.

Ellen faced a mountain of challenges. She would often find herself caught in a loop of tailoring each service to individual client needs. While her intentions were good, it meant hours of extra work, inconsistent pricing and loads of energy spent just trying to keep up.

Upon deeper reflection, Ellen realised that many of her clients, despite coming from different industries, had similar organisational structures and goals. For instance, the arts and cultural centres she worked with, regardless of their specific focus, all had multiple programs and were looking to supplement revenue to meet operating costs. This insight sparked a lightbulb moment for Ellen.

She decided to create fundraising campaign templates that could be applied to all her arts and cultural centre clients, with only minor adjustments needed to suit each centre's specific context. This streamlined approach not only saved Ellen countless hours but also allowed her to offer more competitive and consistent pricing.

Ellen didn't stop there. She also noticed that her most successful and fulfilling projects were with smaller arts and cultural centres. This realisation brought back memories of her younger years, specifically her time as a member of a local community theatre group that provided her with vital emotional support during a challenging period in her life. Ellen felt a deep connection to this type of work, as if she was paying forward the kindness she had once received.

Motivated by this personal connection, Ellen adjusted her marketing strategy to attract more of these ideal clients. She shared her own story, which powerfully demonstrated her authentic passion for giving back to the industry that had once helped her. This vulnerability and genuineness struck a chord with the boutique arts and cultural centres, leading to number of new engagements.

With a more focused client base, Ellen was able to further refine her service offerings. She created a suite of fundraising packages specifically designed for the needs and challenges of smaller arts and cultural centres. This specialisation not only made her work more efficient but also more impactful.

The change in Ellen's business was like night and day. With streamlined packages and a targeted client focus, Ellen saw her revenue increase without the added stress. Her clients appreciated her deep understanding of their sector and her personal commitment to their success. Ellen rediscovered her joy and purpose in her work, knowing she was making a real difference in a field close to her heart.

Through Ellen's experience, we see the power of leveraging patterns and personal passion to create focused, impactful service packages. It's about working smarter by aligning your offerings with your own story and values. That's when the magic really happens.

***

Lessons Learned

Here are the key takeaways from Ellen's path to personal growth:

- **Find Your Niche**

  Focusing on a specific client type that resonated with her own story and values enabled Ellen to create more targeted and effective service packages.

- **Look For Patterns**

  Despite apparent differences, many clients share similar structures, goals or challenges. Identifying these patterns allows for the creation of streamlined solutions that can be adapted to individual needs.

- **Let Your Story Shine**

  Ellen's personal connection to her work with arts and cultural centres made her marketing more authentic and compelling. Don't be afraid to infuse your own narrative and passions into your brand.

- **Specialise For Greater Impact**

  Tailoring her offerings to the specific needs of her ideal client type allowed Ellen to provide more value and make a bigger difference in her chosen field.

- **Align Work With Purpose**

  When Ellen focused on projects that truly mattered to her, work became more than just a job. It became a source of fulfilment and a way to create positive change.

Ellen's development demonstrates that creating powerful service packages isn't just about strategy. It's about heart. When we align our offerings with our own stories and purpose, we can create truly meaningful and transformative work.

***

ACTION STEPS

Crafting a service package that stands out requires thoughtful, deliberate action. Follow these steps to create an irresistible offering:

- Identify your passions and areas of excellence.
- Consider your potential clients' challenges and service expectations.
- Develop a comprehensive service package that showcases your unique strengths.
- Create a detailed plan for supporting clients throughout their time working with you.
- Establish a clear communication strategy for setting client expectations.
- Implement a system for setting and maintaining professional boundaries.
- Develop a pricing strategy that reflects your value proposition and market position.

Ready to go deeper? Download the free bonus collection at: www.packagepromotescale.com/bonus

Step 2 – Test

Picture yourself as the chef at a local eatery known for its regular diners, and you've just developed a new recipe. You've spent time selecting the ingredients, considering their harmony and visualising the delightful reactions of those who taste it. However, before adding it to your restaurant's menu and investing in bulk ingredients, wouldn't you want to know if it truly resonates with the patrons?

Let's consider two scenarios:

1. You add this new dish to your menu without any prior sampling. Some diners try it out of curiosity, but the feedback is mixed. While a few enjoy it, many suggest changes and some don't order it again.
2. Before its official addition to the menu, you offer small tasting portions of the dish to a select group of regular diners. They provide real-time feedback, allowing you to tweak the flavour profile, adjust the ingredients and present a refined version that's more universally loved when it finally makes its grand debut.

Scenario 2 ensures that when the dish is officially launched, it's closer to what the majority of your diners want. Similarly, as you're crafting a new package offering, it's imperative to test it before a fully-fledged launch. This prelaunch testing allows you to gauge interest, ensure alignment with client needs and refine your offering based on authentic feedback.

Your offering may come from your expertise, passion, or a market gap you've spotted. Its success depends on matching what your clients actually need or want. This is where testing comes into play. It's your way of ensuring that your package not only resonates with its intended audience but also genuinely benefits them.

As you take in the feedback, approach it with an open heart and mind. Understand that every piece of feedback, be it glowing praise or constructive criticism, is invaluable. It's a stepping stone, helping you craft a package that's both relevant and sought after. Just as a chef might feel a sting when a diner suggests changing an ingredient, you might feel protective of your package initially. However, if you approach feedback from a learning perspective, you will see every suggestion as an opportunity for refinement and enhancement.

Moreover, your business is not only about the product or service you're offering; it's also about the experience. From the moment a client hears about your package to the moment they decide to invest in it, the process needs to feel seamless, genuine and in sync with your brand. Consistency in messaging and delivery is paramount. The testing step is not a sales conversation or doing the package 'live' but is all about testing your package concepts and inclusions.

As we explore the nuances of testing, keep in mind that it is all about alignment and refinement. It's your chance to ensure your new package offering isn't just another dish on the menu but the one everyone's talking about and eager to try. So, with a keen spirit and a focus on the needs of those you serve, let's perfect that recipe together.

***

ADOPTING A GROWTH MINDSET

Testing a new package offering can stir a mixture of excitement and apprehension in any business owner. It's important to adopt the right mindset in during this process. This mindset, often termed a growth mindset, can make the difference between viewing feedback as a stumbling block or a stepping stone.

Testing a new package offering can bring both excitement and apprehension for any business owner. It's crucial to keep in mind that the right mindset is key during this process. Adopting a growth mindset can be the difference between seeing feedback as a barrier or as an opportunity for growth.

A growth mindset is the belief that abilities and intelligence can be developed through dedication and hard work. It's the love of learning, the resilience in the face of setbacks and the understanding that effort is a pathway to improvement. Here's what it means in practical terms:

- **Embracing Challenges**

  Don't shy away from them. Give them a go! Challenges aren't there to defeat you but to make you stronger and more adaptable. Every challenge faced is a lesson learned, even if the immediate outcome isn't what you had in mind.

- **Persevering In The Face Of Setbacks**

  We all face setbacks. However, it's not the setback itself but how you react to it that counts. Instead of feeling disheartened or thinking about giving up, see setbacks as a chance to adjust and move forward with new insights.

- **Understanding The Value Of Effort**

  Nothing worthwhile comes easy. Recognise that the work you invest in testing and refining your package offering will determine its success. Your efforts today will shape tomorrow's results.

- **Learning From Feedback**

  Think of feedback as a gift. Positive feedback affirms your direction, while constructive criticism can highlight areas that may have slipped past you. Both are precious and pivotal for growth.

A growth mindset is all about perspective. Instead of seeing bumps as obstacles, view them as opportunities to recalibrate and move closer to your goals and your clients' needs.

How do you cultivate this mindset, especially if you've been accustomed to a more fixed perspective that shies away from feedback or change?

Start by grounding yourself in positive affirmations. These are powerful tools that can reshape your thinking patterns. Simple affirmations like 'I can learn and grow from this feedback' or 'Every challenge brings new opportunities' can serve as reminders to stay open and receptive.

Next, take a moment to reframe your perspective on testing. Instead of seeing it as a judgement or critique, view it as a tool. It's a way to better understand your ideal clients' needs. Testing is a bridge that helps to establish and enhance relationships. After all, asking for someone's opinion and genuinely valuing it fosters trust and connection.

As you go through the testing process, keep a few things in mind:

- **Always Remember Your 'Big Why'**

  Why did you create this package offering in the first place? Keeping your core motivation front and centre will help you stay grounded, especially during moments of doubt or uncertainty.

- **It's Okay To Be Vulnerable**

  Admitting you don't have all the possible solutions in your package and being open to learning is a strength, not a weakness. Your clients will appreciate your authenticity and commitment to delivering the best offering.

- **Don't Be Too Hard On Yourself**

  Perfect doesn't exist. Your goal isn't to create a package offering that's flawless but rather one that genuinely meets the needs and desires of your clients. Every step you take, every piece of feedback you receive and every adjustment you make is a step closer to that goal. Progress is better than perfection!

Having a growth mindset is like having a compass. It ensures you're always oriented towards learning, enhancement and success. As you prepare and get excited about the testing phase, adopt this mindset, trust the process and know that it's all part of creating a package offering that resonates deeply with your clients.

***

SETTING YOURSELF UP FOR TESTING SUCCESS

Testing is all about putting your ideas into action and seeing how they resonate in the real world. It's that crucial step before the big reveal where you ensure everything is as flawless as it can be. Setting yourself up for testing success means more than just hoping for the best. It's about strategising, preparing and implementing in ways that make the most of this crucial process. We recommend undertaking testing over a period of two to three weeks. This is enough time to get it done and reduce perfectionism (or procrastination!)

First, know what you're aiming for. You need to have a clear idea of what success looks like for your package. This isn't about guessing. It's about knowing. For instance, decide how many people you want to try your offering or what kind of feedback you're looking for.

Once you've got that down, the second part is to plan your steps. Here's a suggestion on how to organise your plan:

- **Write Down Your Goals**

  This will help you stay focused. If your goal is to have 10 to 12 people provide feedback on your package in a period of two to three weeks, then you'll know exactly what you need to work towards.

- **Decide On The Who, What And When**

  Who will you be testing this offering with? What exactly will they be trying? When will the testing take place? Lock in these details so there are no surprises.

- **Consider In Person Or Online**

  Will you meet people in person or do a virtual meeting to test the package? Some people will be happy to spend 45 minutes online but may not be willing to travel to meet in person.

- **Get Your Tools Ready**

  Are you using surveys? Interviews? Observation? Choose the right tools that will help you gather the information you need.

- **Plan For Feedback**

  Decide how you'll collect feedback. It can be through a simple form or maybe a casual conversation. Just make sure it's easy for people to tell you what they think.

Next, make a checklist. This is very helpful to make sure you don't miss any steps. Here's what you might include on your checklist:

- Prepare your package offering for testing
- Contact potential testers
- Schedule testing dates
- Gather your testing tools (survey forms, recording devices etc.)

Be ready to explain your offering clearly. People need to understand what they're trying out. If they're confused, they might not give the kind of feedback you're looking for.

Alright, so you've planned everything out. It's important to be prepared for all possible outcomes. If things go great, that's fantastic! If not, don't sweat it. Every bit of feedback is a clue on how to make your package better.

Be ready to listen too. And we mean really listen. When testers tell you what they think, pay attention and ask questions if you need to. It's all valuable information.

Here are some key points to keep in mind:

- **Stay Organised**

  Keep all your information and feedback in order. This will save you a ton of time when you're looking back to make improvements.

- **Be Patient**

  Testing takes time. You might not get all your answers right away and that's okay.

- **Stay Positive**

  Keep your energy up. If you're excited about your package, others will be too.

After you've collected all your feedback, take some time to think it over. What did you learn? What can you do better? And, most importantly, what did you do really well?

Then, it's time to tweak your package. Use what you've learned to make it even more awesome. This is what we'll be covering in Step 3 – Refine.

Every bit of effort you put into testing your package is going to pay off. You're not only creating a product; you're enhancing the value for your clients, and that's something to be proud of. Keep at it, and you'll see your package offering get better and better.

SELECTING AND APPROACHING YOUR TEST GROUP

Choosing who gets to try out your new package is like deciding who gets the first taste of the new dish you've created. You want people who can clearly describe their impressions, provide genuine feedback, and tell you if it needs a hint more of this spice or a little less of another.

While you may have many candidates, focus on those aligning with your target audience: current clients who've expressed a need, previous clients who might benefit, and potential clients fitting your ideal profile.

When selecting your test group, aim for a diverse mix within your target audience. Include current clients who've expressed needs your package addresses, previous clients who might benefit, and potential clients who fit your ideal profile.

Potential clients are particularly valuable, as they provide fresh perspectives without preconceptions. Current clients can compare the package to your existing services, while previous clients can assess its potential benefits. This diverse range of testers will give you a comprehensive view of your offering's market appeal and effectiveness.

Once you have your list of potential testers, it's time to approach them. Remember, clarity is your best ally. Clearly define what you want from them and communicate it effectively.

Here are a few things to keep in mind when reaching out:

- **State Your Intentions Clearly**

  Be upfront. If you're seeking feedback on specific components or if you want them to try out your package and give an overall review, make it known. Clear expectations lead to actionable feedback. Use a templated email to communicate clearly what's involved, how long it will take and if they need to prepare anything before your call or meeting. If you're communicating on various platforms, such as a Facebook Business Group or LinkedIn, remind them how you first got in touch.

- **It's Not About Selling**

  This isn't a sales call. It's about understanding and refining your package. Approach it authentically and with a genuine desire for feedback.

- **Give A Little Background**

  Share some information about the package before diving in. Give a brief overview or highlight the main benefits. You want to pique their interest without overwhelming them.

- **Stories Connect**

  Offer examples of challenges your package addresses. This can lead to deeper, more insightful conversations. However, just make sure they are genuine instances and not sales stories.

- **Visuals Can Help**

  If you have a simple visual representation of your offering (such as a 3-phase, 9-step framework!) or a basic flow chart, consider sharing it. Sometimes, a visual or picture can convey more than a verbal explanation.

It's important to be flexible when setting up these discussions. Your package testers are doing you a favour by making time in their busy schedules. Tools like Calendly can be great for scheduling appointments, letting testers pick their preferred time slot. And always, always, respect their time. Start on schedule, end on schedule and make sure they know how grateful you are for their insights.

In the end, the process of selecting and approaching your test group involves more than gathering feedback. It encompasses forging relationships, deepening existing connections and positioning your offering in the best possible light. When done right, it can form the basis for a successful package and help to build lasting business relationships.

Every person you approach is a potential advocate for your brand, a future client or a valuable connection in your network. Approach them with respect, gratitude and openness and you'll set yourself up for more than just testing success. You'll be building bridges for future collaborations and growth. In the long run, that's what it's all about.

* * *

GATHERING INTELLIGENCE

You've got your test group ready, your package prepared, and now it's showtime! But the show isn't complete without an audience and, in this case, your audience's reactions are gold. This is where intelligence gathering comes in. Intelligence gathering is all about listening and observing with intention.

Listening is an art, not just a skill. Everyone hears what is being said but not everyone truly listens. Imagine you're talking to a friend about a new dish you tried at a local restaurant. If they're merely nodding along, they are *hearing* you. If they ask which restaurant it was, what ingredients were used or if you would recommend the dish, then they're *listening*. That's the difference. When it comes to your test group, achieving this deeper level of listening is essential.

Here's what active, intentional listening looks like:

- **Being Fully Engaged**

    When someone's sharing their feedback, give them your full attention. This means no checking emails, no getting distracted by other tasks and definitely no thinking about what you'll have for dinner later. You're in the moment with them.

- **Asking Open-Ended Questions**

  Asking a question such as 'Did you like it?' can get you a simple yes or no response. In contrast, asking 'What did you think about it?' can open a conversation. It allows the person to express their thoughts more freely and provides you with richer insights.

- **Avoiding Interrupting**

  It can be tempting to jump in, especially if someone says something you didn't expect. However, hold off and let them finish speaking. You'll have your chance to respond.

- **Noting Key Points**

  It's easy to forget things, especially when you're in the thick of a discussion. Keep a notebook or digital tool handy to jot down anything significant.

Observing is equally important. You see, sometimes, what people don't say is as valuable as what they do say. Notice the hesitation before answering a question, the spark in the eyes when discussing a particular feature or the slight frown when going through a specific process. These signs can help you gather valuable intelligence.

Here are some observational cues to be aware of:

- **Body Language**

  Do they lean in when discussing something or do they seem distant and disinterested? Body language can often signal interest or lack thereof.

- **Facial Expressions**

  A furrowed brow, a delighted smile or a look of confusion can provide insights into their true feelings, even if they don't voice them.

- **Tone Of Voice**

  Excitement, hesitation, uncertainty or enthusiasm can all be gauged from the way someone speaks.

- **Language**

  What words are they using to describe the problems they are facing? Take particular note of their words so that you can use this when refining and promoting your package.

Keep in mind that intelligence gathering isn't a one-time event; it's a continuous process. As you gather feedback and observe reactions, you'll refine your package. And as you refine your package, you'll need to seek out more feedback. This ensures your offering remains dynamic and relevant to your clients' needs.

Once you've done the listening and observing, it's time for the next crucial step: processing. Revisit your notes and replay conversations in your mind and look for patterns. What did most people like? Where did they face challenges? Were there any surprises?

Be willing to accept that while negative feedback might sting a little, it is invaluable. It shows you where there's room for improvement. Acknowledge it. Similarly, positive feedback, while it feels good, serves as an affirmation, not an end point. There's always more to learn and more ways to grow.

The success of your testing also depends on how effectively you gather intelligence and how well you listen and observe. Approaching this with intention not only improves your offering but also shows a deep commitment to those you serve. This dedication is what ultimately defines excellence and success.

***

MAKING SENSE OF THE RESULTS

The hard work is done. You've selected your test group, crafted your package and collected feedback. You've now got some valuable data at hand. It's a treasure-trove of insights waiting to be explored, and it's going to help you make your offering even better.

Organisation

First things first: organisation. Think of it as setting up your workspace before getting down to a big task. Everything should have its place so you can easily find and use it.

Here's a simple way to go about it:

- **Categorise Feedback**

  Start by putting similar feedback together. Maybe a group of people had similar things to say about the user interface, while others focused on content. Create these 'buckets' of information so you know where to look for specifics.

- **Quantify Where You Can**

  If a majority of your testers said the same thing, note that down. It gives weight to their feedback. For instance, if eight out of ten people found a particular section helpful, that's significant.

- **Highlight Outliers**

  While it's essential to focus on common feedback, don't overlook any distinctive perspectives. These outliers can often provide the most valuable insights.

Once you've sorted your feedback, it's time to dig deeper. Think about why someone might have had a particular reaction. Use the data you've collected to gain a better understanding of their perspective.

Refine and Prioritise

This is where things can get challenging. It's tempting to want to act on every single piece of feedback. However, imagine if a chef changed their dish every time someone made a comment. The dish might lose what makes it special. So, while feedback is invaluable, it's also essential to trust your initial vision.

Here's how you can strike that balance:

- **Prioritise Feedback**

  If there's feedback that the majority of your testers highlighted and which aligns with your goals, it's a good indication that it's something to act on.

- **Assess Feasibility**

  Sometimes, making a change might require significant time or resources. Weigh up the benefits against the cost of making the change. If it's a minor tweak that could make a significant difference, it might be worth the effort.

- **Stay True To Your Vision**

  Remind yourself of the reason you started this journey. Feedback is meant to enhance your vision, not completely change it.

As you're going through this process, know that it's normal to feel a mix of emotions. You might be ecstatic about one piece of feedback and a little disheartened by another. That's natural. The key is not to let emotions drive your decisions but to let them inform your understanding.

Lastly, it's a good idea to follow up with your test group, especially if they'll be involved in further testing. Let them know what changes you've made based on their feedback. It shows that you value their input and are committed to making improvements. Plus, it strengthens the bond of trust and collaboration.

Making sense of the results takes some skill. It requires analytical abilities to understand what the data is saying and a touch of intuition to sense what might be right. Carefully analysing, prioritising, and acting upon feedback allows you to refine your offering into a polished gem, full of clarity and value. The ultimate goal is to serve your audience to the best of your ability, and with the insights you've gained, you're one step closer to achieving that.

***

CELEBRATING THE SMALL WINS

Here's a thought that might surprise you: every step you've taken so far, whether it led to a soaring success or a little stumble, is worth celebrating. Why? Because each one is part of your growth and progress. Think about it. When you started your business, there were many unknowns, but with each step, each decision and each round of feedback, you've been filling in the blanks and painting a clearer picture of where you're headed.

Let's start with the small wins. What are they? Well, they're those moments when something just clicks. Maybe it was when you received positive feedback from a tester, or when you successfully tweaked part of your package based on feedback. These moments might not make headlines, but they're the building blocks of your success.

Here's why these wins are such big deals:

- **Build Confidence**

  Every small win is a confidence booster. It reminds you that you're on the right track, and that the effort you're putting in is yielding results.

- **Create Momentum**

  Consider a snowball rolling down a snow-covered hill. It starts off small but, as it gathers more snow and speed, it grows larger and more powerful. Small wins create that momentum, making each subsequent step a bit easier and more impactful than the last.

• **Reinforce Good Practices**

When something works, it's a sign that you're doing things right. Recognising and celebrating those moments reinforces these good habits.

Next, consider the lessons learned. These are not the moments when everything went perfectly. Instead, they're the times when things didn't go as planned. But guess what? These moments are just as valuable, if not more so, than the small wins. Here's why:

• **Growth Opportunities**

Every hiccup or challenge offers a chance to learn and grow. Each one might highlight areas that need a bit more attention or a different approach.

• **Perspective Shift**

Sometimes, it's easy to get tunnel vision and focus only on the end goal. When something doesn't go as expected, it can give you a fresh perspective and maybe even spark a new idea.

• **Build Resilience**

Facing challenges and coming out stronger on the other side? That's resilience. The more you encounter and overcome these moments, the more resilient you become.

So, how can you go about celebrating these wins and lessons? It doesn't always have to be a big, grand gesture. Here are some ideas:

• **Take A Moment**

Whenever you hit a milestone or learn something new, just pause. Reflect on what you've achieved or learned. Feel the accomplishment.

- **Journal It**

  Keeping a journal of your progress can be really enlightening. Jot down the wins, the lessons and your thoughts. Over time, you'll see how far you've come.

- **Share With Your Team**

  If you're working with others, celebrate together. It could be as simple as a group chat shout-out or a virtual high five.

- **Treat Yourself**

  Did you reach a significant milestone? Maybe it's time for that treat you've been eyeing. It's good to reward yourself now and then.

Every step you take brings you closer to your vision. The small wins light the way, and the lessons learned make sure you're on the right path. Celebrate them all. They are all markers of your dedication, hard work and commitment to excellence. After all, it's not only about the destination; it's also about enjoying and learning from the process.

*** *

CONCLUSION

Creating something new and offering it to the world is not only about the end product. It's a process where you continually refine, learn and grow. Throughout this process, several underlying principles have served as your foundation.

- Openness and adaptability have been at the forefront, reminding you to welcome feedback and adjust accordingly.
- Clarity has been your guide, shaping your steps and decisions, and keeping you aligned with your goals.
- Resilience has provided the strength you need to face challenges and come back even stronger.

Active listening and observation skills will prove invaluable, helping you deeply understand user needs and wants.

Celebrating your progress is essential for motivation and as an acknowledgment of your hard work and dedication.

The respect and gratitude you show towards your testers highlights the importance of valuing those who contribute to your progress. At the heart of it all, staying rooted in your purpose ensures that your offering remains genuine and true to your vision.

Throughout this step, there have been recurring themes that tie everything together:

- **Adaptability**

  This is the importance of being flexible and willing to make necessary changes based on genuine insights and feedback.

- **Purposeful Direction**

  While it's crucial to adapt and change, it's equally vital to have a clear vision and direction to keep you focussed.

- **Valuing Feedback**

  More than merely words, feedback is a tool for growth. Treating it with importance and valuing those who offer it has been a consistent emphasis.

- **Resilience And Growth**

  Recognising that setbacks are natural and using them as stepping stones, rather than stumbling blocks, helps with improvement.

- **Relationships**

  Understanding that success isn't achieved alone and that valuing and building relationships, especially with testers, is key to long-term success.

The core themes and principles we've explored aren't just strategies on paper; they're practical guidelines for any consultant aiming to build a lasting impact. They remind us of the significance of adaptability in a dynamic business environment. They champion the value of clear direction, ensuring we move forward with intention.

The emphasis on feedback serves as a testament to its power in shaping effective offerings. Embracing resilience underscores the reality that growth often comes hand in hand with challenges. And the focus on relationships? It's a beautiful reminder that the most meaningful successes aren't just about what we accomplish, but about the people we share them with and the relationships we build along the way.

Keep the values we've discussed at the core of your foundation, providing a strong base from which any consultant can confidently and humbly approach their work. These values are more than just words. They serve as a guide, directing your actions and decisions as a distinguished consultant.

***

CASE STUDY

Amy, a passionate communications consultant in the social impact sector, was developing a new package for her clients. She had high hopes but wanted to be certain her offering was just right before reaching out to her network.

Amy faced numerous challenges, especially when it came to creating her stakeholder engagement package. Setting up the testing phase felt like an uphill battle. Despite her desire to test her package effectively, Amy found it difficult to structure her test sessions. Her mindset wavered too. Instead of viewing feedback as growth opportunities, Amy often internalised it, leading to bouts of self-doubt.

Determined to overcome these hurdles, Amy took a step back and reassessed her approach. She started by clearly defining her testing objectives, focusing on the specific aspects of her package that needed validation. This clarity helped Amy design more targeted and effective test sessions.

Next, Amy worked on her mindset. She began to view feedback as valuable insights rather than personal critiques. This shift allowed her to approach the testing phase with a more open and curious frame of mind, ready to learn and improve.

To select the right participants, Amy carefully considered who was in her network, identifying individuals who closely matched her ideal client profile. She reached out to them with personalised invitations, clearly explaining the purpose and value of their participation. When approached in this way, individuals felt respected and understood the significance of their input.

During the test sessions, Amy focused on creating a safe and engaging environment that encouraged honest feedback. She actively listened to participants' experiences, asking probing questions in a respectful manner to uncover deeper insights.

After gathering the feedback, Amy took the time to analyse the data. She looked for patterns and recurring themes, using this information to improve her package. She adjusted the content, structure, wording and delivery based on the insights gained.

The impact of these changes was remarkable. Amy's refined package resonated strongly with her target audience, addressing their specific pain points and desires. The improved offering not only attracted more clients but also led to higher satisfaction and glowing testimonials.

On a personal level, Amy found renewed confidence and excitement in her work. Embracing the testing process as a growth opportunity not only improved her package but also helped her develop a more resilient and adaptable mindset.

***

Lessons Learned

On the following page you'll find the key takeaways from Amy's path to personal growth…

- **Set Clear Testing Objectives**

  Defining specific aspects to validate allows you to design more focused and effective test sessions.

- **Embrace A Growth Mindset**

  View feedback as an opportunity to learn and improve, rather than a personal critique.

- **Choose The Right Participants**

  Carefully select test participants who closely match your ideal client profile for the most relevant insights.

- **Create A Safe And Engaging Environment**

  Foster open and honest feedback by creating a supportive atmosphere during test sessions.

- **Actively Listen And Probe Deeper**

  Go beyond surface-level feedback by asking probing questions to uncover valuable insights.

- **Analyse And Look For Patterns**

  Take the time to thoroughly analyse the feedback, identifying recurring themes and patterns to guide your refinements.

- **Make Strategic Adjustments**

  Use the insights gained to make targeted improvements to your package's content, structure and delivery.

Amy's story demonstrates the value of conducting a testing phase and doing it well. Approaching it with clarity, openness, and a commitment to growth enables you to refine your offerings to better serve your clients and achieve greater success and fulfillment in your work.

***

ACTION STEPS

Testing your package is crucial for ensuring its success. Here are some action steps to guide you through the process:

- Define specific objectives and measurable outcomes for your testing phase.
- Develop a strategy to prepare mentally for the testing process.
- Ensure you have the tools and resources you need for your testing sessions.
- Establish the criteria and a process for selecting ideal test participants.
- Develop a structured approach for engaging with your test group and gathering feedback.
- Use active listening techniques for both verbal and non-verbal cues.
- Maintain momentum and commitment throughout the testing process.
- Keep test participants informed of your progress and learnings.
- Analyse and categorise the feedback you receive.

Ready to go deeper? Download the free bonus collection at: www.packagepromotescale.com/bonus

Step 3 – Refine

Congratulations on designing and testing your package! That initial step of crafting your package and bringing it to the point of testing is a commendable feat. The real magic often lies in the next step: refinement.

To truly make your package shine, it needs those fine-tuning moments. This is when you look at what's working, what's resonating with your audience and ask yourself: How can this be even better? Whether it's simplifying a process, tweaking the presentation or ensuring it all aligns with your heartfelt vision, refinement is where your offer goes from good to great.

Here are a few essentials to consider:

- **Reflect On Your 'Big Why'**

  Your passion and vision have brought you this far. Using them as your compass can offer clarity as you refine your offering.

- **Knowledge Of The Landscape**

  Understand where your package sits in comparison to others and seek out your points of difference.

- **Authenticity Is Pivotal**

  It's not about delivering a polished performance but rather

ensuring your message connects deeply.

- **Feedback Is Gold**

  Welcome it, engage with it and let it guide you to those impactful tweaks and shifts.

- **Stay Nimble And Open To Learning**

  Even the most established and mature offerings can benefit from fresh perspectives and updates.

Refinement isn't reinvention; it's enhancement. You've laid a strong foundation and now it's time to polish and adjust your package, ensuring it isn't just another option for clients but one that genuinely stands out, resonates with them and reflects their needs.

It's time to embrace refinement with enthusiasm, harnessing the feedback and insights you receive to create an offering that truly stands out.

***

REVIEWING AND INTEGRATING FEEDBACK

Now that you've got a grip on your feedback, it's time to roll up your sleeves and put those insights to work. The goal here isn't just to make changes, but to make the right changes that will elevate your package to new heights. So, let's start turning feedback into actionable refinements.

Remember those trends you spotted during the feedback analysis? They're going to be what guides you through this step. Start by addressing the most recurrent themes in the feedback. Often, these are the areas where making a change will have the greatest impact. For instance, if most of your audience found a specific segment confusing, refining that segment will benefit the largest number of users.

Keep in mind that just because multiple people mentioned a particular point doesn't automatically mean a total revamp is necessary. Sometimes, a subtle tweak or a slight shift in presentation can make all the difference.

Regarding those outliers: While they weren't the majority, they still matter. Some of these distinctive perspectives may have touched on aspects you hadn't considered before. While it's not necessary to address every single outlier, use them as a lens to view your package from different angles. Ask yourself: Is there a broader underlying issue that this feedback hints at?

When integrating feedback, consider the following points:

- **Action With Intention**

  Before making a change, always ask: How does this enhance the value of my package? Every refinement needs a clear purpose that aligns with your primary goal.

- **Simplify To Clarify**

  We've touched on this before, but it's essential to reiterate. In your eagerness to address feedback, don't complicate matters. If there's a straightforward way to incorporate a change without compromising its effectiveness, always take that option.

- **Check For Unintended Ripple Effects**

  When you tweak one part of your package, it might inadvertently affect another part. Be vigilant and ensure that your changes don't disrupt other elements that are working fine.

- **Don't Give Away The Farm**

  You don't have to put everything into the one package. Think about ways you can create mini packages, mini workshops or digital templates as upsells or down-sells. Always be mindful of the client experience and avoid overwhelming them along the way. Confused people don't buy, and overwhelmed clients are unlikely to get the results they want.

Feedback integration is an ongoing process, not a one-time event. After refining your work based on initial feedback, revisit the feedback to ensure you've addressed the core issues, going beyond superficial changes. This helps confirm that your refinements truly meet the needs of your target audience.

Throughout the integration process, use the feedback you received to guide your improvements without losing sight of your original goals. When refining your package, remember that you're actively working to better serve your target audience. Each refinement brings your package closer to achieving your mission and meeting the needs of those you want to help.

***

ENHANCING THE CORE COMPONENTS

Alright, let's look at making your package even more awesome than it already is. Imagine you've got a cool backpack. Now, what's it filled with? The essentials, of course! That's just like the core components of your offering. These are the things your clients absolutely love and come back for, time and again.

Start by knowing the essentials inside out. What gets your clients excited about what you have to offer? And is there something they're wishing for that you haven't put in yet? You've got the necessary elements in the main compartment of the bag and now you're looking for any extra pockets or gaps. If you spot one, think about how you can fill it in a way that adds value without overloading the backpack.

Sometimes, it's beneficial to offer something extra. Like if you're on a hike, wouldn't it be nice to have a pair of binoculars? That's what upsells and cross-sells are. They're the 'binoculars' that give your clients an even better view. Not everyone on the hike will need them, so it's alright to charge a bit extra for these special add-ons.

Staying current is a must. How do you do that? Keep a pulse on what's happening in your world. Just like you'd update your playlist with the latest tunes, you need to refresh your offering with what's new and in demand. Regularly dig into what's trending in your industry and tweak your package to stay one step ahead.

Don't feel compelled to integrate every new idea into your package. Be thoughtful and choose enhancements that resonate with your clients and won't diminish the effectiveness of your offering.

The cherries on top of your package are the extra touches that, while not essential, enhance the overall offering. Think of them as additional tools or services you provide to amplify the impact of your work. Just as strategic partnerships can elevate the success of a community initiative, these add-ons can strengthen your service. However, too many add-ons can overwhelm your clients and dilute the focus of your core offering. Consider offering different levels of extras, like a basic, pro, and deluxe version of your package. Each level provides different benefits, allowing people to choose what suits them best without the fear of missing out.

As you enhance your package, here's a quick checklist to keep things on track:

- **List The Must-Haves**

  These are the things your clients can't do without.

- **Scout For The Gaps**

  What's missing that could make a big difference?

- **Add With Purpose**

  For every new feature, ask if it makes the package better.

- **Stay In The Know**

  What's new in the market that your clients would love?

- **Make It Special**

  Consider those special add-ons that give extra value.

Keep it simple, keep it valuable and keep it exciting. With every tweak and addition, you're making sure that your package isn't just a collection of things but a well-thought-out set that's perfect for your clients. It's like packing for a trip. You want everything to be just right. Take a step back, look at your offering and make it the best it can be – not by stuffing it with everything under the sun but by carefully selecting each item to make sure it's exactly what your clients need.

***

STREAMLINING THE SERVICE DELIVERY PROCESS

So, you've got this fantastic package that your clients are excited about. Great job! The key lies not only in what you deliver but also in how you deliver it. Think about getting a parcel delivery. Isn't it so much better when it arrives quickly, is neatly wrapped and maybe even has a thank-you note inside? That's what we're exploring here: making sure your service delivery is as smooth and delightful as the content of your package itself.

Efficiency

Consider the impact of efficiency on your business. When everything runs like a well-oiled machine, you save time and resources and your clients get a seamless experience. It's like when you go to a store and there's a clear sign showing you where everything is. You just feel more at ease, right?

To achieve this, start by mapping out each step of your service delivery. From the moment a client comes on board to the final follow-up, write down every little detail. It might sound tedious but this is going to be a lifesaver. With a clear path in front of you, it's easier to spot any bumps or roadblocks.

Once you've mapped out your process, look for any repetitive or unnecessary steps. Perhaps there's a form clients repeatedly fill out that could be automated, or maybe multiple emails could be consolidated into one. Consider using short, prerecorded videos to support clients during the onboarding process, and share cloud-based folders for file uploads to eliminate double handling. Streamlining these steps makes the process smoother for everyone involved.

Communication

Effective communication is the backbone of any thriving business. It's the key element that keeps everything flowing. When clients know what to expect and when to expect it, they're more likely to trust the process and stick around for the long term. Always keep them in the loop. A simple update can work wonders in building that bond and reassuring them that they're in good hands.

What about the unexpected bumps? Things don't always go according to plan and that's to be expected. What matters is how you handle these situations. This is where flexibility comes into play. While having a set process is great, the ability to adapt when needed can save the day. If a client has a very specific need or there's a sudden change in the plan, being able to pivot ensures that the ball keeps rolling without any hiccups.

One effective strategy is to leverage tools and technology. There's an abundance of apps and platforms available which are designed to make service delivery easier. Whether it's scheduling meetings, automating tasks or managing projects, there's likely a tool that can help you streamline the process. We cover this in more detail in Phase 3: Scale.

Alright, let's recap some of the key points:

- **Map Out The Process**

  Know each step of your service delivery like the back of your hand.

- **Trim The Excess**

  Remove any unnecessary or repetitive steps to save time and resources.

- **Communicate, Communicate, Communicate**

  Always keep your clients informed. They'll appreciate it.

- **Be Flexible**

  When the unexpected happens, be able to adapt and keep things moving.

- **Use Tools**

  There are tons of resources out there designed to help you. Take advantage of them.

Keep in mind that while the content of your package is super important, the way you deliver it plays a massive role in how it's received. It's like having the best ingredients for a meal but not cooking it correctly or presenting it well – it loses its charm. Streamlining your service delivery ensures that your clients are getting the value they signed up for, as well as having a delightful experience along the way. And when that happens, you're not only delivering a service; you're building lasting relationships.

***

FINE-TUNING YOUR OFFER

Here, we need to consider promises. In business, your offer is like a promise you're making to the market. It's a commitment that says, *This is what you can expect from me.* And, just like any other promise, it's essential to ensure that we can deliver on it, right?

Promises aren't set in stone. As we learn and grow, it's natural to adjust and fine-tune our offers to better serve clients. Consider how your favourite pizza place might have changed its recipe over time, perhaps adding new toppings or tweaking the crust. Not because the old pizza was bad, but because they found a way to make it even better. Similarly, fine-tuning your offer ensures you're consistently delivering the best possible value.

Listening is essential. It's one of the simplest things to do, yet it is so powerful. Listen to your clients, your peers and even your competitors. They could offer valuable insights that can shed light on areas of your offer that might need a little tweak. Feedback is like little breadcrumbs leading you towards a better, more refined promise.

Be sure to stay rooted in authenticity as you sift through this feedback. It's easy to get swayed by every little suggestion or to mirror what everyone else is doing. While it is essential to stay relevant, it's equally important to ensure that your offer remains a genuine reflection of your values and what you stand for.

Don't be afraid to experiment. It's good practice to test out new things and see how they resonate with your audience. Maybe you've traditionally offered one-on-one sessions but you're considering group sessions. Give it a shot! Trying different approaches gives you a clearer picture of what fits best for both you and your clients.

Clarity is crucial. A well-defined offer serves as a clear roadmap, directing potential clients to your business. Ensure your offer is straightforward and easy to understand. You want people to read it and immediately think, *Oh, I get it. This is exactly what I need!* If they're left scratching their heads, unsure of what you're offering, it might be time for some fine-tuning.

Here are some pointers to keep in mind:

- **Listen Actively**

  Pay attention to feedback and use it as a guide to make necessary adjustments.

- **Stay Authentic**

  While progress is good, ensure that your offer remains true to your core values.

- **Experiment Boldly**

  Don't shy away from trying new things. You never know what might click.

- **Be Clear**

  Ensure that your offer is straightforward and easy for potential clients to understand.

Refining your offer is an ongoing process. What worked wonders a year ago might not have the same impact today. Staying alert and receptive to change is the name of the game.

In the end, it's all about ensuring that your promise to the market is clear, valuable and consistently delivered. Because when you make a promise, you're building trust. And by fine-tuning your offer, you're saying, *I care about giving you the best.* And that's a message everyone appreciates.

***

DOES YOUR PRICING STACK UP?

A topic that's on many people's minds when they think about their business is pricing. Now, don't get us wrong, we know talking money can feel a bit daunting, but setting the right price for your package is like finding that sweet spot on the volume of your car stereo. Not too loud, not too soft, but just right.

Pricing isn't about plucking a number out of thin air. It's a balance of understanding your worth, knowing your market and ensuring that your business thrives. Even though you're passionate about what you do, at the end of the day, your business needs to make sense financially.

So, how do you make sure of that?

- **Revisit Costs Regularly**

  Things change. The cost of materials, tools or even the rent for your workspace can fluctuate. Keep an eye on these costs. If they've increased and you haven't adjusted your prices, you might be short-changing yourself (affecting your ability to be profitable and remain viable) without realising it.

- **Check Out The Competition, But Stay True To You**

  It's good to know what others are charging but don't fall into the trap of just copying them. You bring something unique and special to the table. Your prices need to reflect your value, not merely what others are doing.

- **Value Your Time**

  Time is, quite literally, money. Consider the hours you put into delivering your package. Are you pricing in a way that respects the time and effort you invest? If you find yourself working around the clock and not seeing the returns, it's a sign to re-evaluate.

- **Listen To Client Feedback**

  Have clients ever mentioned they would've gladly paid more for the value you provide? On the flip side, if potential clients are consistently turning away due to price, you might want to investigate further.

- **Be Flexible**

  Pricing doesn't have to be rigid. You can have promotional prices, seasonal discounts or loyalty programs. These can help to attract new clients and reward loyal ones, all while making good business sense.

After crunching the numbers and arriving at a new price, it's natural to feel a bit nervous about rolling it out. You might wonder, *What if my clients don't see the value?* or *What if they go elsewhere?* But remember, those who truly value what you offer will be willing to invest in it. And there's deep satisfaction in working with clients who genuinely appreciate and value your expertise.

However, let's not change prices on a whim. Keep your clients in the loop. If you decide to adjust your pricing, communicate the reasons clearly. Perhaps you're offering additional services, or maybe your costs have risen. Honesty goes a long way. When clients understand the reasons behind a price change, they're more likely to be on board.

Revisiting your pricing strategy deals with more than the numbers. It involves understanding your value, being confident in it and ensuring that your business remains sustainable and profitable. It's like a regular health check-up but for your business's finances. So, go ahead and give your pricing the attention it deserves. After all, your work is worth every penny, and it's essential to make sure that your pricing reflects that.

***

ACKNOWLEDGING THE CONTRIBUTIONS

Imagine that you're working on a puzzle and someone hands you a crucial piece that brings the whole picture together. That's kind of what your test group does for you. They give you those missing puzzle pieces, the insights that help your package become more refined, understandable and valuable. It's like teamwork, where everyone has a role to play and each contribution is crucial.

When someone assists us, our instinctual reaction is to say, 'Thank you.' This section focuses on acknowledging and expressing gratitude to your test group for their invaluable input.

One thing is clear: a simple 'thank you' is more powerful than we often realise. It's not just good manners; it signifies appreciation and recognition of the value someone brings to the table. When people feel acknowledged and appreciated, they are more likely to engage in future collaborations. They feel connected to the process and the bigger picture, creating a win-win situation for everyone.

So, how can you go about this acknowledgment?

- **Send Personalised Thank You Notes**

  In today's digital age, a handwritten note stands out. Taking the time to personally thank each participant shows them that their contribution was meaningful. If snail mail isn't your thing, a personalised email or Loom video can also do wonders. The key is to make it personal, showing them that you remember and value their specific input.

- **Share The Impact**

  Imagine you gave feedback but never knew if it mattered. It would feel like shouting into a void. Instead, give your test group a glimpse of the changes and refinements you made based on their insights. By doing this, they can see the tangible impact of their contributions.

- **Publicly Acknowledge Them**

  With their permission, do a shout-out on social media with a quotable quote and link to their organisation or business. This is a great way to generate interest in your new package and share your acknowledgement to a broader audience.

- **Engage Them In Future Projects**

  What better way to show your appreciation to someone than by inviting them to be a part of future projects? It tells them that you value their perspective and would love to have them onboard again.

- **Give Exclusive Offers Or Discounts**

  As a token of appreciation, consider offering the participants special rates or early bird access to your refined package. It's a small gesture that says, *Hey, thanks for being a part of this. Here's a little something for you.*

- **Create A Feedback Wall**

  If you have a physical office space or even a digital platform, consider setting up a space where you showcase some of the most impactful feedback. It's a constant reminder of the community that's helping to shape your offering.

- **Host A Thank-You Event**

  If resources allow, you could host a small gathering, a webinar or even a digital meet and greet. It's a chance to interact, share stories and deepen the bond.

Further, acknowledging the contributions of the test group also does wonders for you. Each time you say thank you, it's a reminder of the collaborative effort, the community that supports you and the shared vision you're working towards. Plus, fostering these relationships is vital. Today's test group participant could be tomorrow's brand ambassador, spreading the word about your fantastic package.

Acknowledgment is about building and nurturing relationships. Your test group has offered you their time, insights and, sometimes, even a fresh perspective you hadn't considered. They've played an instrumental role in shaping your package. And while their primary aim might not have been recognition, a heartfelt acknowledgment goes a long way. It's a simple yet effective way to say, *I see you, I value you and I appreciate you*. And who doesn't love to hear that?

***

CONCLUSION

Now, it's time to review our progress. You started with a package—an idea you believed could make a difference. Through the process of refining, that idea has begun to take a shape that's clearer, sharper, and more focused on what your clients truly need.

Refining isn't just about making things better; it's about understanding and connecting. It's about making sure that what you offer speaks directly to the hearts and minds of those you're looking to serve. Think of it as tuning an instrument. The process doesn't change what's at the heart of the music, it just makes every note ring true and clear.

Together, in this step we've:

- Taken the feedback and used it as a spotlight, highlighting the areas where we can make our package even more awesome.
- Looked at our package's core components and made sure each one is strong and valuable.
- Stayed up to date with the latest and greatest in our field, ensuring we offer something that works today and is ready for tomorrow.
- Thought about all the extra goodies we could add to make our package stand out.
- Looked at the way we deliver our package, making the whole process smooth and enjoyable for our clients.
- Polished our promise to the market, ensuring that what we're offering is beyond a product or a service; it's a commitment to excellence.
- Revisited our pricing to ensure that what we're doing makes sense for our clients and for our business too.
- Taken time to thank those who've contributed to our progress, knowing that their insights have been priceless.

Through all these steps, you've probably learned a lot. Not only about your package, but about yourself, your business and the people you're aiming to help. It's these learnings that will keep you standing firm when new challenges come. And they will come, but that's just part of the adventure, isn't it?

Refinement is a continuous process. The world changes, trends shift and new needs emerge. Your package will need to adapt.

Keep your ears open to feedback; keep your eyes on the horizon; and always, always, keep your mind open to change.

While it's important to look ahead, it's just as important to be present. Enjoy the process, celebrate the small wins and learn from every step. This package you've poured your heart into is more than just a part of your business; it reflects your dedication to your craft and your commitment to serving others.

In the end, what matters most is the impact you make. It's not only about the package you've created but the difference it makes in the lives of those who use it. So, keep refining, keep improving and keep reaching out. Stay curious, stay eager and, above all, stay true to your vision. Your package is more than a product or a service; it's a bridge between you and the people you serve, a bridge built on understanding, care and genuine value.

***

CASE STUDY

Mark, a business planning consultant, took the exciting step of crafting a new service package. After diligently testing it with a select group from his target market, he was ready to refine his offering. However, this step proved trickier than he had anticipated.

Mark encountered a few specific challenges during refinement. Firstly, the feedback he received from his test group was inconsistent. Some participants raved about certain elements of the package, while others questioned their value. This lack of consensus made it difficult for Mark to figure out which elements were essential.

Additionally, Mark struggled with information overload when researching industry trends. The sheer volume of information he uncovered left him feeling overwhelmed and unsure of how to effectively integrate new ideas into his package.

To overcome these challenges, Mark decided to take a structured approach. He began by organising the feedback he had collected, categorising it based on common themes and the specific aspects of the package it addressed. He achieved this efficiently by using sticky notes grouped on a wall. This helped him identify the most critical areas for improvement.

Next, Mark approached us for some mentoring support. In a single session, he gained valuable insights into which elements of his package were likely to be most impactful for his target audience. This external perspective helped Mark prioritise his efforts to refine his package.

To tackle the information overload challenge, Mark set aside dedicated time each week to review industry trends. He compiled a list of the most relevant and reputable sources, focusing on quality rather than quantity. Breaking this into manageable chunks allowed Mark to stay informed without becoming overwhelmed.

As Mark implemented these changes, he also made a point of regularly seeking feedback from his clients. He created a simple survey that he sent out after each engagement, asking for their thoughts on the package. This ongoing feedback loop allowed Mark to continuously iterate and improve his offering.

The impact of these refinements was significant. Mark's clients expressed greater satisfaction with each engagement, acknowledging his services felt more tailored to their specific needs. They appreciated the clarity and focus of the revised offering, which made it easier for them to understand the value they were receiving.

On a personal level, Mark found the refinement process very rewarding. In taking a structured approach and seeking out targeted feedback, he gained a deeper understanding of his own expertise and how best to serve his clients. The refined package not only improved Mark's business outcomes but also increased his confidence and satisfaction in his work.

***

Lessons Learned

Here are the key takeaways from Mark's path to personal growth:

- **Organise And Categorise Feedback**

  Systematically organising feedback based on themes and specific package elements allows you to identify the most critical areas for improvement.

- **Seek External Perspective**

  Engaging with trusted mentors or industry experts can provide valuable insights and help you prioritise your refinement efforts.

- **Manage Information Overload**

  Setting aside dedicated time for research and curating a list of the most relevant and reputable sources can help you stay informed without becoming overwhelmed.

- **Implement An Ongoing Feedback Loop**

  Regularly seeking feedback from clients allows for continuous iteration and improvement of the service package.

- **Embrace The Personal Growth**

  The refinement process not only improves business outcomes but also deepens your understanding of your own value and how best to serve your clients.

Following Mark's example and applying these lessons enables you to create service packages that deliver greater value to your clients and bring you greater satisfaction in your work.

***

ACTION STEPS

Refining your package is an ongoing process that requires focused attention and effort. Follow these steps to continuously improve your offering:

- Establish a schedule for regular package and pricing reviews and updates.
- Utilise external perspectives on your package.
- Review and analyse past client interactions.
- Analyse your competition to identify improvement opportunities.
- Keep abreast of industry trends and best practices.
- Brainstorm value-adding features.
- Consider creating tiered package options.
- Acknowledge and thank contributors to your refinement process.
- Reflect, celebrate and recognise your progress and growth.

Ready to go deeper? Download the free bonus collection at: www.packagepromotescale.com/bonus

Phase 2: Promote

Once you've crafted your specialised service packages in the Package phase, it's time to start promoting them. This means more than merely spreading the word. Promotion is also about making sure that the clients who reach out are the ones you want to work with. In this phase of the Package Promote Scale Framework, we'll address and reframe limiting beliefs that often stop consultants from using simple but effective sales and marketing strategies. The goal is to build a strong and qualified pipeline full of real opportunities. These are the clients most likely to move forward and who align with your values and way of working. By mastering this phase, you'll take control of your business, choosing your clients and shaping your own success.

Step 4 – Attract

At the core of every interaction, there's a desire to connect. Whether it's between two friends catching up or a consultant addressing a client's need, the foundation is the same: attracting and forming a bond based on trust and understanding.

So, how do you become that person others seek out? It begins with storytelling. People are more inclined to remember stories than mere facts. When you share experiences of the successes you've had or challenges you've overcome, it resonates. It gives others a glimpse of what they can expect from you and provides them with a clearer picture of your expertise and dedication.

Sharing your successes allows you to demonstrate capability. When others hear about the positive impact you've had or the transformations you've been a part of, it builds confidence. It offers reassurance that you're making promises that you're delivering on.

Being genuine plays a massive role in attraction. Authenticity is magnetic. It means showing that you genuinely care about a person's needs and goals. When you take the time to understand someone, to dig deep into their aspirations, they notice. And that genuine interest is what differentiates a passing interaction from a meaningful connection.

Effective communication is crucial, and today we have many tools at our disposal, from face-to-face meetings to digital platforms. Using these tools wisely and adapting to the needs of your audience ensures that your message is clear, understood and impactful.

Then there's feedback, a crucial component of growth. Without understanding what you're doing right and where you might be going astray, progress is challenging. Welcoming feedback and actively seeking it out positions you in a cycle of continuous improvement.

Lastly, believe in yourself and your abilities. There's confidence in recognising your strengths and leveraging them. When you exude confidence, others notice and, more importantly, they believe in your ability to help them.

Attracting clients into your sphere isn't a one-time action. It's an ongoing process where you build connections, earn trust, and prove your value. It's about being a reliable partner, rather than fulfilling a need.

PART 1

CRAFTING YOUR ORIGIN STORY & ELEVATOR PITCH

Everyone has a story. It's that series of events and experiences that have shaped you, driven you, and brought you to where you are today. Just as superheroes have origin stories that define who they are and why they do what they do, so do you. And it's time we give it the attention it deserves.

Your origin story goes deeper than where you were born or what school you went to. It's about those pivotal moments that changed the direction of your business. Maybe it was a client who challenged you to think differently, a course that opened your eyes to new possibilities, or a business mentor who guided you toward a breakthrough. Perhaps it was a project that stretched your skills in unexpected ways or a lesson learned from a setback that ultimately propelled you forward. These are the moments that set you apart and shape the way you serve your clients.

Imagine being at a gathering. People are chatting, exchanging pleasantries, and then someone asks, 'So, what do you do?' This is where your elevator pitch comes into play. Instead of simply stating your job title, you have a concise and compelling response that encapsulates what you do and why you do it.

Crafting An Effective Elevator Pitch

An elevator pitch is a brief, engaging summary of what you do and the value you provide. A strong elevator pitch should be:

- **Concise**

  Keep it under 30 seconds to maintain interest.

- **Clear**

  Use simple, jargon-free language that a non-expert could understand.

- **Compelling**

  Highlight what makes you unique or different.

- **Conversational**

  Deliver it naturally, not like a memorised script.

A basic elevator pitch structure follows these elements:

1. **Who You Are And What You Do**

   Start with a brief introduction to your role or area of expertise.

2. **The Problem You Solve**

   Describe a challenge or need your target audience faces.

3. **Your Solution And Unique Value**

Explain how you help solve this problem.

4. **A Call To Action Or Engagement**

Invite the listener to continue the conversation, ask a question, or take the next step.

Example Elevator Pitch

Consider an example of a consultant working with social enterprises on their project planning:

> *"Hi, I'm Alex, a consultant specialising in strategic planning for social enterprises. Many mission-driven organisations struggle to turn their big ideas into concrete, actionable plans. I help them create clear roadmaps and impact-driven strategies so they can stay focused on making a difference. I'd love to hear about the projects you're working on—what's your biggest challenge right now?"*

Let's break this example down into its individual elements:

1. **Who You Are And What You Do**

"Hi, I'm Alex, a consultant specialising in strategic planning for social enterprises."

2. **The Problem You Solve**

"Many mission-driven organisations struggle to turn their big ideas into concrete, actionable plans."

3. **Your Solution And Unique Value**

"I help them create clear roadmaps and impact-driven strategies, so they can stay focused on making a difference."

4. **A Call To Action Or Engagement**

"I'd love to hear about the projects you're working on—what's your biggest challenge right now?"

Together, these elements create a natural, engaging pitch that clearly communicates your role, the problem you address, how your work provides meaningful value, and a way to move things forward.

Crafting Your Own Elevator Pitch

Start by jotting down key moments in your journey—experiences that shaped your perspective and passion. Identify the core problem you solve and why it matters. Then, practice refining your pitch until it feels authentic and natural.

Key Tips:

- **Be Genuine**

  Share real experiences and passion for what you do. *This helps build trust and make your pitch memorable.*

- **Stay Focused**

  Avoid overwhelming details—stick to the core message. *This allows your listener to quickly grasp your value.*

- **Practice And Refine**

  Test your pitch with friends or colleagues and adjust based on feedback. *This ensures it flows naturally and resonates with different audiences.*

- **Speak With Confidence**

  Believe in your story and the value you bring. *This inspires trust and makes your message more compelling.*

Crafting your origin story and elevator pitch is about understanding yourself better, recognising your value, and learning to communicate it effectively. It's an activity that will not only set you apart but will also draw others to join you on your path.

***

SHOWCASING SUCCESS STORIES AND TESTIMONIALS

Imagine that you're scrolling through your favourite social media platform. Among the countless photos and status updates, you spot a post from someone sharing a personal win. They're excited, they're grateful, and they're giving a big shout-out to someone who helped them achieve that success. It catches your attention, doesn't it? That's the magic of client success stories and testimonials.

As a consultant, your value is often demonstrated by what you've achieved for others. People want to know you can deliver on your promises, and they assess this through stories about the individuals and companies you've helped in the past.

Sharing these success stories and testimonials on your socials is an excellent strategy for multiple reasons:

- **Trust Building**

  When prospective clients see that others have benefited from your expertise, it boosts their confidence in you. They start to wonder, *If they did it for them, then maybe they can do it for me too.*

- **Human Element**

  Stories are relatable. They remind everyone that behind every business transaction, there's a human component, a personal journey.

- **Visibility**

  With the algorithmic nature of most social platforms, content that engages gets seen more. More eyes on your content means more potential business.

But there's an art to doing this effectively, and on the next page you'll find some best practices to consider…

- **Get Permission**

  Before you share any success story or testimonial, always get written consent. You want to ensure that your client is comfortable with their story being out in the public domain.

- **Be Authentic**

  Don't just put up a clever quote. Share a bit about the journey. Where did they start? Where are they now after your guidance? Authenticity shines through, and people can tell when things are genuine.

- **Use Visuals**

  If your client is okay with it, include photos or even short video clips. A before-and-after picture or short video testimonial can be impactful. Visual elements often convey messages more powerfully than words alone.

- **Engage**

  When people comment on your post, thank them, answer any questions they might have or just engage in a friendly chat. Social media is, after all, meant to be social!

- **Mix It Up**

  Ensure you're not only posting testimonials. Variety is the spice of online life. Share other content too, so your feed doesn't become monotonous.

Here's something to chew on. When you showcase your client's success, it's not merely a pat on the back for you. It's a beacon for others who are in the position your client was before they met you. It signals hope, possibility and a pathway to similar success.

Every time you help a client reach a milestone, solve a complex issue or achieve a goal, it's a golden opportunity. Not only for you, but for the countless others out there who might be facing the same challenges.

So, the next time you finish a consulting project and your client is beaming with pride and gratitude, think of all the other people who might benefit from hearing about it. Genuine stories of transformation and progress always stand out. They're the little pockets of inspiration that many people enjoy coming across. And, as a consultant, they're your most powerful endorsements. Always cherish them, share them and let them be the testament to the meaningful work you do

How to Write a Compelling Story: Adopting a Storytelling Structure

Stories are an integral part of the human experience and are an indispensable tool for consultants to communicate, engage and inspire others. So how do you craft a compelling story—especially when it comes to showcasing a client's success?

Here's a structure you can adopt for your client success stories:

Story Structure

a. A **CLIENT** – Who is the main character?
b. With a **GOAL** – What do they aspire to achieve?
c. Has a **PROBLEM** – What's stopping them?
d. Finds a **SOLUTION** – What is the key to solving their issue?
e. Takes **STEPS** to implement it – How do they go about using this solution?
f. Faces **CHALLENGES** along the way – What obstacles do they face?
g. Achieves an **OUTCOME** – How does it all end?
h. Learns a valuable **LESSON** – What insight did they gain from this journey?
i. Is **BETTER OFF** now – How has their situation improved?

Here's how this could translate into a story you can share with potential clients:

a. Alex, a client of mine who had just stepped into the role of general manager at a thriving social enterprise,

b. wanted to breathe new life into the organisation and get the volunteer workforce passionate and motivated again.

c. However, he encountered a disengaged volunteer base, with dwindling participation rates and low morale. This led to several projects stalling and community initiatives suffering.

d. Eventually, Alex found the core issue wasn't a lack of passion, but a lack of clarity and direction.

e. He began organising regular feedback sessions, clear communication channels and appreciation events.

f. But Alex faced challenges such as initial resistance from some long-term volunteers wary of change and logistical hiccups in organising community events.

g. However, with patience, reassurance and persistence, volunteer participation rates began to soar, and the energy was palpable.

h. This helped Alex realise the importance of clear communication, recognition and the power of inclusivity.

i. Since then, the social enterprise has witnessed higher volunteer engagement and successfully launched multiple community projects that had been previously stalled.

Harnessing the art of storytelling, especially by focusing on the client's journey, can be a game changer for you as a consultant. Not only does it humanise the challenges and solutions, but it paints a vivid picture that prospects can relate to, putting them in the shoes of a past client and allowing them to envision their own success.

These narratives capture attention, evoke emotions and build trust. Putting the client at the forefront of the story and showing the transformation they underwent with your guidance subtly highlights your expertise without the hard sell.

This storytelling approach can resonate deeply with people, making your services memorable and increasing the likelihood that potential clients will be drawn to what you offer.

Storytelling Guidelines

In crafting your client success stories, it's worth taking into consideration the following to achieve the maximum impact:

- **Personal Touch**

  The story must focus on an individual, not an entity. This helps in making the story relatable and personable.

- **Spotlight On The Client**

  Recognise that the client is the main character of this tale, not you. You play a guiding, supporting role.

- **Relatability Is Key**

  The person you're narrating about needs to be someone your listener can easily connect with. This could be because they're in a similar boat or they see parts of their own journey reflected in the client's story.

- **Highlight The Challenge**

  The problem the client faces needs to be significant. It's what will draw your audience in, making them eager to know how it was overcome.

- **Your Role**

  The solution you provide needs to be something you can also offer to your listener. You're showcasing how you can help.

- **The Obstacles**

  The road to success isn't usually smooth. Emphasise the hurdles faced along the way. This not only makes the tale more gripping but also amplifies the satisfaction when success is achieved.

- **Favourable Outcome**

  Detail the end results and the wisdom the client gained. Ideally, this part depicts a positive change, indicating the client's growth and betterment through the process.

With these guidelines, crafting a compelling story becomes an efficient process. It's a blend of art and technique. And every time you share it, remind yourself that it's more than just a story. It's a testament to growth, resilience and the positive change that you, as a consultant, bring into someone's life. Keep telling stories! As one of our mentors, Andrew Griffiths, says in a simple yet powerful way: *'Stories good. Tell lots.'*

***

GATHERING AND LEVERAGING INTELLIGENCE

Imagine for a moment that you're heading to a place you've never been. You could wing it and take random turns hoping you'll get there, or you could get a map, learn about the terrain, and make informed decisions that will get you to your destination faster and more efficiently. The world of consulting is much like this process. And the map? That's the valuable intelligence you gather and leverage. It's about knowing the landscape of your clients' worlds, understanding their challenges, and having the right information at your fingertips to guide them effectively.

So, what exactly do we mean by valuable intelligence? Simply put, it's any piece of information that can give you a clearer understanding of your client's situation, industry trends or potential challenges. Think of it as your secret weapon, something that gives you an edge in providing the best service possible.

Here's how you can gather and leverage this information:

- **Know Your Client**

    First and foremost, get to know your client. What are their goals? What obstacles are they facing? Take time to sit down with them, have a chat and really listen. It's the little details that often make the biggest difference.

- **Stay Updated**

  Industries shift, technologies advance, and market dynamics change. Make it a habit to stay up to date with the latest news, trends, and innovations related to your client's field. This can be as simple as subscribing to industry newsletters, attending webinars or joining professional groups online.

- **Leverage Feedback**

  After every project or consultation, ask your clients for feedback. What went well? What could have been done differently? This not only helps you improve but also shows your clients that you value their opinion.

- **Network, Network, Network**

  Your network is a treasure-trove of insights. Engage with your peers, attend industry events and join discussions. You'd be surprised at how much you can learn just by listening to the experiences of others.

- **Document Everything**

  This might sound tedious but it's essential. Maintain a system where you document all the information you gather. It can be as simple as a digital notebook or a more sophisticated customer relationship management (CRM) system. This ensures that all your hard-earned intelligence is easily accessible when you need it.

Gathering intelligence is only one side of the coin. The real magic happens when you leverage it. Here's how:

- **Tailored Solutions**

  Equipped with the right information, you can craft solutions that are tailored to your client's needs. Instead of a one-size-fits-all approach, your strategies will be as individual as the challenges they address.

- **Stay Ahead Of Problems**

  Understanding industry trends and potential challenges allows you to anticipate problems before they arise. This proactive approach can save your clients time, money and a lot of headaches.

- **Build Trust**

  When clients see that you're well-informed and always have the latest information at your disposal, they're more likely to trust you. And in the world of consulting, trust is everything.

- **Refine Your Strategies**

  Use the feedback and insights you gather to refine your strategies and offerings continuously. It's a cycle of improvement that ensures you're always at the top of your game.

Gathering and leveraging valuable intelligence keeps you on track and helps you take steps that are informed and intentional. While it might seem like a lot of work initially, the results are well worth the effort. Your clients will not only benefit from your in-depth understanding and insights but will also see the genuine commitment and passion you bring to the table.

***

TAKING STOCK OF YOUR NETWORKS

Imagine that you've engaged a party planner to help arrange a big get-together you intend to host. Before the invitations can be sent out, you'd need to make a list of all the people you know — family, friends, neighbours, classmates, co-workers and so on. Some you talk to often, while others you may only connect with once a year, but each person on that list holds an important place in your life. Understanding and nurturing your diverse connections can bring immense value to your business and life. Let's explore how you can take stock of your networks.

Everyone you know or have interacted with forms a part of your network. It's like a giant web where each strand is a connection. Here are some steps to help you get a clearer picture:

- **Make A List**

  Start by writing down the names of people you've worked with, met at conferences or connected with online. Don't forget about those you've met in informal settings too, like a friend's birthday party or a community event.

- **Categorise Thoughtfully**

  Group these people based on how you know them. Are they past clients? University friends who are now in similar fields? Knowledgeable professionals you met at a workshop? Doing this gives you a clearer understanding of the different circles you belong to.

- **Recall The Last Interaction**

  When was the last time you talked to each person? What did you discuss? Keeping this in mind can help you identify who you might want to reconnect with or give a friendly update about your work.

- **Identify Mutual Benefits**

  Think about how you can help each other. Maybe one of your contacts is looking for a service you provide or perhaps they offer something you need. Recognising these mutual benefits strengthens the bond.

- **Keep It Genuine**

  Every relationship involves a mutual exchange. It's about what you can gain and about how you can support, help or simply be there for others.

Having this list is just the starting point. Like an effective community organiser who builds relationships, understands the needs of the community, and fosters open communication, your network also requires regular attention and care. Nurturing these connections ensures that your work continues to have a meaningful and lasting impact. Here's how:

- **Check-In Regularly**

  Drop a message or make a call. It doesn't always have to be work-related. Maybe you read an article you think they'd like or perhaps you just want to see how they're doing.

- **Share And Celebrate**

  Did you achieve something notable? Or maybe they did? Celebrate those wins. Share it with your network. It fosters a sense of community and shared growth.

- **Seek And Offer Guidance**

  Are you facing a challenge? Reach out. Your network might have insights or solutions. Similarly, be available when someone from your circle needs advice.

- **Engage Online**

  Interact with their content online. Leave a comment on their blog, share their post or give a thumbs up to their updates.

- **Attend Events**

  Even if it's a virtual coffee catch up, make an effort to attend. It's a great way to keep the connection alive and to meet new people.

- **Stay Updated**

  If someone from your network shares a professional update, like a job change or a new project, make a note. It helps in keeping conversations relevant and shows that you're genuinely interested in their progress.

Lastly, it's worth noting that while it is great to have a vast network, it's even more vital to have a meaningful one. Quality over quantity, as they say. Every person you connect with contributes their own distinct perspective, experience, and value. Taking stock of your networks not only organises your contacts but also acknowledges and appreciates the rich tapestry of relationships that support, challenge, and enrich your professional life. It's these connections that often lead to growth opportunities, collaborations or simply valuable lessons. So, take a moment, reflect on those connections and cherish them. After all, in the field of consulting, it's often the people you encounter who make all the difference.

***

ENCOURAGING WORD-OF-MOUTH REFERRALS

Have you ever excitedly told your friends about a new eatery in town, a book you couldn't put down or a movie that kept you on the edge of your seat? That genuine excitement to share a great find with someone else is word of mouth in action. And guess what? It's an incredibly powerful tool not only for movies and books but also for you in your business.

Starting with the basics, word-of-mouth referrals occur when someone recommends your consulting services based on their positive interactions. The best part? These referrals come free of charge but carry a weight worth its value in gold. Why? Because a recommendation from a trusted individual can influence decisions more than any social media post or advertisement.

So, how do you encourage these word-of-mouth referrals? Here are some steps to guide you:

- **Do Exceptional Work**

  This might sound obvious, but it's the foundation on which these referrals are based. When you consistently deliver outstanding results, clients will naturally want to sing your praises.

- **Build Strong Relationships**

  Beyond the work itself, people remember how you made them feel. Be genuine, listen to your clients and show them that you truly care about their success.

- **Ask For Feedback**

  After completing a project, ask your clients for feedback. This not only helps you improve but also opens a door for them to express their satisfaction. And when they vocalise it, they're more likely to share that positive sentiment with others.

- **Remind Them To Spread The Word**

  Sometimes, all it takes is a small nudge. If a client praises your work, thank them and say something like, 'I'm so glad you're happy with my work! If you know anyone else who could benefit from my services, feel free to pass on my details.'

- **Stay In Touch**

  Even after a project wraps up, keep the communication lines open. Check in occasionally, share updates or news and let them know they're on your mind. When you're in their thoughts, you're also more likely to come up in relevant conversations they have with others.

- **Create Shareable Content**

  Whether it's a thoughtful LinkedIn post, an insightful article or an engaging video, creating content that people find valuable makes it easier for them to share your expertise with their network.

- **Recognise And Thank Referrers**

  If someone does refer you, ensure you thank them. This could be by way of a simple note, a little token of appreciation or a phone call. This small act can encourage them and others to continue referring in the future.

While working on these steps, it's crucial to understand the significance of trust in this process. The power of referrals lies in the authenticity and trust they carry. When someone refers you, they're putting their own reputation on the line by vouching for you. The person trusting the referral is placing confidence in both their friend's judgment and in you. It's like a chain of trust, where every link matters. Consistently being reliable, maintaining integrity, and delivering excellence ensures that this chain remains unbroken.

Quality matters. One deeply satisfied client sharing their insights with a handful of trusted peers can be more effective than numerous casual mentions.

Finally, while word-of-mouth referrals are fantastic, they shouldn't be your only source of new business. They're a part of the puzzle, complementing other strategies you employ.

As a consultant working within sectors where competition is high and choices are many, being the name that comes up in conversations can be a game changer. Focusing on genuine relationships, maintaining your commitment to excellence, and occasionally giving a gentle nudge in the right direction makes you the consultant everyone's excited to recommend. After all, there's no better stamp of approval than a satisfied client telling their peers, 'You have to work with them!'

SPEAKING AT EVENTS

Imagine you're attending a conference. You grab a seat, the room buzzes with excitement, and as the lights dim, a person walks onto the stage. The next hour captivates you. The speaker isn't just talking; they're sharing, engaging and connecting with everyone in that room. And as they wrap up, you think, *I need to learn more about what they do.*

That's the power of speaking at events.

Being a speaker doesn't just put you in the limelight; it positions you as an authority in your field. It's a chance to share your knowledge, showcase your expertise and connect with potential clients or partners. Whether you're on a panel discussion, taking a hot seat session, energising a crowd as an emcee or delivering a thought-provoking keynote, each platform offers a valuable opportunity to make an impact.

So, how can you step onto that stage and leave an indelible mark? Here are a few ways:

- **Know Your Audience**

  Before you even start crafting your talk, think about who you're speaking to. What are their interests, challenges and expectations? When your message resonates with them, they're more likely to engage and remember it.

- **Prepare And Practise**

  It might sound basic but the importance of preparation cannot be stressed enough. Once you have your content, practise it. Practise in front of a mirror, record yourself or present to a friend. The more you practise, the more confident you'll feel.

- **Engage And Interact**

  The best sessions aren't just monologues; they're dialogues. Ask questions, invite comments or even include short activities. This interaction helps to break any monotony and strengthens the connection with your audience.

- **Share Real Stories**

  People remember stories better than plain facts. Share real-life examples, successes or even failures that offer valuable lessons. It makes your content relatable and memorable.

- **Stay Authentic**

  In a world full of rehearsed speeches, genuine authenticity stands out. Be yourself. If you're passionate about a topic, let it show. If something is close to your heart, share it. Authenticity builds trust.

- **Use Simple Language**

  Not everyone in your audience may be familiar with industry jargon. Stick to simple language, ensuring your message is clear and understandable for everyone.

- **Offer Value**

  Aim to provide actionable insights or solutions that your audience can implement. When they find value in your talk, they're more likely to seek you out afterwards.

Speaking at events also comes with added benefits. For starters, it's a wonderful networking opportunity especially if your ideal clients are in the room. After your session, you'll likely find attendees approaching you for a chat, with a question or even with a business proposition. And don't forget about the ripple effect. People share impressive sessions with their networks, extending your reach beyond just the attendees.

Moreover, speaking engagements enhance your credibility. They give you a platform to not only talk about what you know but to demonstrate it also. And as you consistently deliver insightful sessions, event organisers might even seek you out, offering more opportunities.

However, it's not about self-promotion or selling from the stage. Yes, speaking at events can benefit you, but your primary focus remains on delivering value to your audience. That's the heart of it all. Being sincere in your intent to share and help naturally draws people towards you.

So, next time you spot an opportunity to speak, welcome it. It might feel daunting, especially if it's your first time, but the rewards are well worth the effort. Over time, with each event, you'll refine your style, gain confidence and grow your audience. And who knows? You might just be the speaker captivating the next person walking into that conference room, leaving them thinking, *I need to learn more about what they do.*

PART 2

CREATING AN ONLINE PRESENCE

Let's look at your online presence. This is your digital playground where you can showcase who you are and what you do. While some may think it's all about posting selfies or what you had for lunch, it's much more than that. It's about making connections, sharing your story, and yes, having a bit of fun along the way.

Think about the last time you heard of someone interesting. What's the first thing you did? If you're like most folks, you probably looked them up online. That's why having an online presence is so important. It's often the first impression you make, and you want it to be a good one.

Here are some tips on where to begin:

- **Start With A Website**

  Even a basic website can do wonders. It's a central hub where people can find crucial information about you. This includes your packages, contact details, client success stories, testimonials and perhaps a blog where you share valuable insights. Keep it updated, user-friendly and easy to navigate.

- **Engage On Social Media**

  Platforms like LinkedIn, YouTube and even TikTok can be valuable. You don't need to be everywhere; just pick one or two platforms where you feel your clients spend their time. Share helpful content, engage in conversations and use these platforms to connect and establish your expertise.

- **Consistency Is Key**

  Whatever platforms you choose, be consistent. If you start a blog, try to update it regularly. If you're on social media, engage daily or weekly. A consistent presence tells potential clients that you're active and invested in your field.

- **Stay True To You**

  Your online presence needs to reflect who you are and what you do. It's fine to share personal triumphs or interesting events from your daily life. It adds a human touch and makes you more relatable.

- **Interact, Don't Just Broadcast**

  The online world isn't just a space for you to talk *at* people. It goes both ways. Respond to comments, answer questions and engage with other people's content as well.

- **Learn And Adapt**

  The digital world is constantly changing. What works today might be outdated tomorrow. Keep an eye on trends, learn from others and don't be afraid to tweak your approach.

Having an online presence is about building relationships, showing your expertise and being a part of a community. It's like planting a garden. You have to keep watering it, pulling out the weeds and adding a bit of fertiliser occasionally. When you do, it grows, blooms and might just bear fruit when you least expect it.

Take time to plan your content and look for ways to repurpose it on various platforms such as using a transcription tool like Rev or Loom to transcribe audio content into blogs.

Think about a popular YouTube star, TikTok creator or Instagram influencer you're familiar with. What makes them so compelling? It's probably got a lot to do with them allowing themselves the freedom to be who they are or to play the role they're portraying. That level of comfort shows up as congruence. It's the state you want to achieve when you're not second guessing yourself, but rather allowing yourself to show up without the least bit of uncertainty about who you are, what you stand for and the value you add to the world around you.

Get out there. Be genuine. Be consistent. And most importantly, be yourself. Your online presence reflects who you are, and when done right, it can open doors to opportunities you never even knew existed. In a digital world, the connections you make are still very real. They can be the difference between being just another name online and being someone who truly stands out.

***

GUESTING ON PODCASTS

Have you ever listened to a podcast? They're convenient audio programs that you can download and listen to anytime, anywhere. And guess what? Being a guest on one can be a big win for you. It's like having a friendly chat that lots of people get to listen in on. Plus, it's a chance to share what you know, meet new people and let others discover how awesome you are at what you do.

So, how do you get started with being a guest on podcasts? Here are some steps you can take:

- **Find The Right Fit**

  Look for podcasts that discuss topics you're knowledgeable in. There's no point in talking about baking cakes if you're all about playing guitars, right? Once you find a good match, you'll know you're talking to people who are actually interested in what you have to say.

- **Reach Out**

  Send a friendly message to the podcast host. Tell them a bit about yourself and why you think you'd be a great guest. Make sure to let them know what you can discuss that their listeners would love.

- **Get Ready To Talk**

  If a podcast host says yes, do your homework. Know what

the show is about and plan what you want to say. You don't have to write it all down, but having some points in your head can help.

- **Tell Your Story**

  On the podcast, share your experiences. People love to hear about real-life stuff—the good, the bad and everything in between. It makes you relatable and can make what you're saying really stick with them.

- **Be Clear And Concise**

  When you're talking, keep it simple. You want people to understand and remember your message. Cut out the complicated words and keep your sentences short and sweet.

- **Listen And Engage**

  Conversations need to flow in both directions. Listen to the host and respond to what they say. Focus on building a connection rather than simply getting your message out.

- **Follow-Up**

  After the show, express your gratitude to the host. This not only shows your appreciation but also keeps the door open for future opportunities. The host might invite you back for another interview, recommend you to other hosts or even promote your work on their social media channels.

- **Spread The Word**

  When your podcast episode comes out, share it with everyone. It's your moment in the spotlight, so let people know.

- **Stay In Touch**

  Keep in contact with the host and their listeners. Answer any questions that come your way and be part of the community. You never know; they might recommend you to other podcast hosts.

Being a guest on podcasts can be fun and rewarding. You get to talk about what you love and you never know who might be listening. It could be a future client, someone with a cool opportunity or just a new fan of your work.

Consider that every time you're on a podcast, it's like leaving a little piece of yourself out there in the world for people to find. You're sharing your knowledge and leaving clues about who you are and what you can do for others. And the more podcasts you're on, the more clues there are for people to follow that lead right back to you.

Take the leap and get your voice out there. Podcasts are a powerful way to reach new ears. And anything is possible. The next person to hear you might just be the one you've been hoping to connect with all along. It's all about talking, sharing and connecting, and when you do it right, it's like opening doors without even knowing where they might lead. Be your genuine self, and have a good time with it. That's what really makes a lasting impression.

***

HOSTING WEBINARS AND WORKSHOPS

Alright, let's explore another fantastic way you can share what you know and connect with people: hosting webinars and workshops. Think of webinars as online classes or presentations where you're the teacher and workshops as more hands-on sessions where everyone rolls up their sleeves and gets involved.

Some of you might be thinking: *I'm not tech-savvy enough* or *I don't think I'm interesting enough to hold people's attention*. If you've got something valuable to share, there's an audience out there eager to hear it.

Starting With Webinars

Here's what to keep in mind:

- **Pick Your Topic**

  What do you know inside out? What topic can you speak about with passion? That's your starting point. It needs to be something that you not only love but also helps solve a problem for your audience.

- **Plan Ahead**

  Jot down what you want to cover. It doesn't need to be a script, but having a rough plan can help you stay on track. When nerves kick in, having some notes can be a lifesaver.

- **Choose Your Tech**

  There are lots of platforms out there to help you run webinars. Some are free; some come with a cost. Do a little homework to find what suits you best.

- **Promote It**

  Let people know about your webinar. Share it on social media, send out emails and tell your friends and family. The more, the merrier!

- **Engage With Your Audience**

  During the webinar, make sure you're not just talking at people. Ask questions, run polls or encourage them to chat among themselves. This keeps things lively and interactive.

Running In-Person Workshops

Use these tips to set yourself up for success:

- **Decide On The Format**

  Will it be a half-day event? Just a few hours? Or maybe even a full weekend? You decide the most suitable type based on the depth of what you're covering and what your audience can commit to.

- **Gather Materials**

  Depending on your topic, you might need certain tools or materials. Make a list and ensure everything is ready before you begin.

- **Engage Participants**

  This is all about interaction. Make sure everyone is involved. Maybe have them work in pairs or perhaps give them meaningful tasks. Keep them active and engaged.

- **Invite Feedback**

  After the workshop, ask participants for feedback. It helps you learn, improve and grow. Plus, it's a great way to understand what your audience really wants.

Why Do This?

Hosting webinars and workshops can seem daunting, but they're a brilliant way to share your expertise. You're directly helping people, answering their questions and building strong connections. Plus, these events position you as an authority in your field. Consider how to use recorded webinars as 'evergreen' content so that people can watch them on demand after registering. Use them to build your email list so you can communicate directly with offers, news and events.

Imagine the ripple effect when people discuss your webinar or workshop with their friends, colleagues and family members. As word spreads, more and more people become familiar with what you do. It's like planting a seed that grows into a tree, branching out in all directions.

The main goal is to provide value. Whether it's teaching a new skill, giving insights or offering a fresh perspective, it's all about bringing something beneficial to your audience.

Go on, give it a shot! Deliver your first webinar or workshop. As you host more and more, you'll become more comfortable and might even start to love it! It's a wonderful way to meet new people, share your passion and make a genuine impact.

***

CONCLUSION

We've covered a lot of ground, from the importance of crafting your story to the power of testimonials, public speaking, and establishing a robust online presence. We've also explored the benefits of utilising podcasts and webinars.

Now, it's time to reflect on the core motivations that brought you here. While attracting clients is an important goal, it's more profound than that. It's about making a meaningful impact, sharing your expertise, and genuinely helping those in need of your services. Keeping these central aims at the heart of your actions is essential for creating a consulting practice that is not only successful but also fulfilling and impactful.

There are a few core truths to hold onto:

- **People Connect With People**

  Before strategies or fancy tools, it's the human connection that truly counts. Always bring your authentic self to the table. Let people see the real you, with all your quirks, passions and experiences. That's what makes you relatable and what will make others want to work with you.

- **Consistency Is Your Best Friend**

  No matter which route you choose to connect with potential clients, do it consistently. If it's webinars, host them regularly. If it's social media, post often and engage with your followers. This constant presence builds trust and showcases your dedication.

- **Value Comes First**

  Before any sale or agreement, think about the value you can provide. It's easy to get caught up in the rush of gaining new clients, but taking a step back and ensuring you're genuinely benefiting them will lead to longer, more rewarding relationships.

- **Feedback Makes You Stronger**

  Never shy away from feedback, whether positive or negative. Both have their value. Praise boosts your morale and shows you what you're doing right, while constructive criticism paves the way for growth and development.

- **Never Stop Learning**

  New tools emerge, trends change, and the needs of clients shift. To stay ahead, you must be a continuous learner. Invest time in improving yourself, exploring new methods, and refining your skills.

- **Relationships Over Transactions**

  Every client you work with isn't just a transaction or a contract. You're in a relationship with them. Build that bond, nurture it and see how it leads to not only business growth but personal enrichment too.

- **Enjoy The Journey**

  While the destination – attracting clients – is important, the journey you undertake, with all its ups and downs, teaches you the most. Throughout the process, welcome every challenge, celebrate every win, learn from every setback and enjoy every moment.

As we wrap up this step, we hope you feel equipped, inspired and ready to implement what you've learned. Success doesn't happen overnight. With determination, passion and the key principles we've outlined, success is within reach.

***

CASE STUDY

Sasha, a consultant passionate about diversity and inclusion, crafted a new package and hoped the right clients would naturally gravitate towards it. She put up a few posts about it on her LinkedIn profile and even mentioned it in one of the LinkedIn groups she was a part of, but it didn't lead to any genuine interest. Sending out emails to a few of her contacts also only brought in lukewarm interest. It was a far cry from the client list Sasha was hoping for. Deflated, she felt like she was shouting into a void.

One of the main challenges Sasha faced was attracting clients who truly valued her expertise in diversity and inclusion. Many potential clients seemed to be more focused on ticking a box than genuinely embracing change. Additionally, Sasha struggled to differentiate herself in a crowded market where many other consultants claimed to offer similar services.

Determined to overcome these hurdles, Sasha took a step back and reassessed her approach. She realised that to attract her ideal clients, she needed to showcase the transformative impact of her work and draw upon her own insights.

Sasha began by gathering testimonials from past clients who had undergone significant cultural shifts thanks to her guidance. She crafted compelling client success stories that highlighted the specific challenges each organisation faced and the measurable results they achieved through her diversity and inclusion initiatives.

Next, Sasha revamped her online presence. She updated her website with a clear, compelling message that spoke directly to her ideal clients. She showcased her case studies prominently and shared thought-provoking articles that demonstrated her expertise.

Sasha also leveraged the power of storytelling. She began sharing her journey, her personal encounters with exclusion as a person with a disability and the discrimination she faced that drove her passion for diversity and inclusion. Showing her vulnerability and connecting with her audience allowed Sasha to build trust and establish herself as an authentic voice in the field.

To expand her reach, Sasha investigated speaking opportunities at industry events and conferences. She tailored her presentations to address the specific challenges faced by her ideal clients, offering practical insights and strategies they could implement immediately.

The impact of these changes was profound. Sasha's authentic, story-driven approach resonated with her target audience. Her website traffic increased as did her engagement on LinkedIn, and inquiries from potential clients began to pour in. She found that the individuals and organisations reaching out to her were of a different quality. They were no longer just looking to tick a box but were genuinely committed to creating inclusive cultures.

As Sasha's client base grew, she found herself working with organisations that truly valued her expertise. The work was more fulfilling and the results were more impactful. Sasha's business began to flourish, and she became a sought-after voice in the diversity and inclusion space, attracting her ideal clients in the process.

***

Lessons Learned

Here are the key takeaways from Sasha's path to personal growth:

- **Showcase Transformative Impact**

  Highlight case studies and testimonials that demonstrate the specific, measurable results clients have achieved through your work.

- **Craft A Clear, Compelling Message**

  Ensure your online presence and marketing materials speak directly to your target audience and clearly articulate the value you offer.

- **Leverage The Power Of Storytelling**

  Share your own journey and the experiences that drive your passion for your work. Vulnerability builds trust and authenticity.

- **Seek Out Targeted Speaking Opportunities**

  Present at events and conferences where your ideal clients gather, offering practical insights and strategies that address their specific challenges.

- **Attract Clients Who Value Your Expertise**

  Focusing on attracting the right clients makes your work more fulfilling and your impact more significant.

Sasha's story shows that by authentically sharing your expertise, telling your story and focusing on the transformation you offer, you can attract clients who are the right fit for your consultancy and the impact you want to create.

***

ACTION STEPS

Attracting your ideal clients requires a strategic and proactive approach. Here are some practical steps you could take:

- Craft and tailor your elevator pitch.
- Collect and share client success stories and testimonials.
- Stay attuned to industry trends.
- Nurture and maintain existing relationships.
- Encourage client referrals.
- Build credibility through speaking engagements.
- Create a strong online presence.
- Increase your visibility through podcast appearances.
- Showcase your expertise through webinars.

Ready to go deeper? Download the free bonus collection at: www.packagepromotescale.com/bonus

Step 5 – Connect

You've laid the groundwork with an enticing service package that's drawing people in. They're intrigued by what you offer and are leaning in closer for a better look. So, where do we go from here? How do we transform this initial interest into deep, lasting connections?

Well, think about it this way. Have you ever felt the magic of a true connection? It's that special spark when you meet someone new and, within moments, you feel like you've known them forever. It's also that deep understanding with a longtime friend where words become unnecessary and a mere glance says it all. Connections like these are invaluable, both in our personal lives and in our professional ventures.

In our day-to-day lives, we interact with countless people. We chat with the barista while grabbing our morning coffee, exchange pleasantries with neighbours or engage in small talk at social events. However, how many of these interactions turn into genuine connections?

Running a consultancy can be lonely, especially if you are a solo entrepreneur. Connecting is a great way to enrich your business and yourself.

Building real, lasting relationships is more than talking. It's about understanding and being understood. Just like in a dance, both partners need to be in sync. It's not merely about stepping forward but ensuring that your partner is right there with you. Connecting is a skill that can be acquired, developed and refined. It takes practice, understanding, patience and intent.

Here are some of the reasons why we seek to connect:

- **Explore New Horizons**

  Every person we meet knows something we don't. Connecting opens doors to new ideas, perspectives, and opportunities.

- **Build A Strong Network**

  More than how many people you know, genuinely connecting with others refers to how deeply you know them. Quality always triumphs over quantity.

- **Access To Resources And Knowledge**

  A strong connection might introduce you to a world you didn't know existed. This could open doors to new ideas, insights and opportunities that can broaden your horizons and support your growth.

- **Spot Potential Collaborations**

  Genuinely connecting with others allows you to recognise synergies and possibilities for future projects or collaborations.

At times, we might feel a bit shy or out of our comfort zone when trying to connect, especially in new or unfamiliar settings. Every deep connection once started as a simple hello. It's alright if not every interaction turns into a lifelong bond, but it's essential to be genuine and authentic in every attempt.

True connections require mutual respect, trust and understanding. They flourish when we actively listen, share our truths and show up as our authentic selves. It's more than just an exchange of business cards or a follow on social media. It's about investing time, effort and emotions into understanding another person and letting them understand you.

By the end of this step, we hope you'll see the beauty and power of genuine connections and be inspired to foster them in every facet of your life. Because, just like a melody that stays with you long after the song ends, a true connection leaves an imprint on your heart, creating moments of magic and memories to cherish.

***

CULTIVATING THE CONNECTION MINDSET

Building genuine connections extends beyond a technique, strategy or some secret handshake. It means cultivating the right mindset. Imagine your mind as a garden. If you want to see beautiful blooms, you don't just toss some seeds around and hope for the best. You prepare the soil, water the plants and tend to them regularly. Similarly, forging strong connections with others requires nurturing the right attitudes and behaviours. Some people identify as either an ambivert or omnivert. An ambivert always displays a healthy mix of introversion and extroversion. Omniverts face extremes in introversion and extraversion and, unlike ambiverts, have trouble balancing outgoingness and shyness. Cultivating a connection mindset aligned with who you are and your values is a game changer.

Openness

Picture a door. If it's always closed, nothing can enter or exit. Similarly, in our interactions, if we're not open to new ideas, perspectives or feedback, we risk missing out on valuable insights.

Being open means:

- Accepting that we don't know everything.
- Being willing to change our perspective based on new information.

- Recognising that every person we meet has something valuable to teach us, even if it's not immediately apparent.

Recognise that being open doesn't mean agreeing with everything. It's about giving every idea a fair chance.

Genuine Interest

Think of a magnet. It attracts objects without saying a word. In the same way, when you show genuine interest, people naturally gravitate towards you. Cultivating genuine interest means:

- Asking the deeper whys rather than just skimming the surface.
- Remembering details from past interactions, showing you truly listen.
- Fully engaging when someone speaks, putting aside distractions.

Expressing genuine interest doesn't make you nosy. It shows that you are truly valuing the stories and perspectives of those you interact with.

Empathy

Empathy allows you to mirror the emotions of those we connect with. To be empathetic means:

- Truly attempting to step into someone else's shoes.
- Feeling *with* them, not *for* them.
- Responding in a way that acknowledges how they are feeling.

Empathy reminds you that every client or colleague has their own story, and taking the time to understand that story is invaluable.

Authenticity

Being authentic is about being our true selves, and involves:

- Not trying to be someone else or putting on a façade.

- Communicating honestly, even when it's challenging.
- Ensuring our actions align with our words.

People connect with realness. When you're genuine, others can sense it and are more likely to trust you.

Curiosity

If you were anything like us as a kid, you probably asked 'why' a lot. That curiosity is at the heart of an eagerness to learn, understand, and explore.

Being curious involves:

- Asking questions, even if they seem basic.
- Not settling for the surface answer but digging deeper.
- Approaching challenges as puzzles waiting to be solved.

In the world of consulting, curiosity helps you uncover the root of a problem or the heart of an opportunity. It drives you to look beyond the obvious and seek out the underlying causes, the hidden patterns and the unseen connections.

Wonder

Approaching with a sense of wonder is about valuing the complexity and depth of our networks, our clients and their challenges. Cultivating a sense of wonder when connecting deeply with others involves:

- Pausing to genuinely reflect on the diverse range of insights and backgrounds each person brings.
- Cherishing the intricacies of every business model, recognising that every piece plays a part in the grander scheme.
- Embracing the unexpected twists in a client's narrative and using them as stepping stones to forge even stronger connections.

Viewing our interactions and engagements through a lens of wonder not only connects us but also celebrates the richness of every story and perspective.

Consistency

Consider the sunrise. Every day, without fail, it shows up. Similarly, consistency in your actions and behaviours lets others know they can rely on you.

Consistency means:

- Keeping your promises and commitments.
- Delivering a steady quality of work, time after time.
- Ensuring others know what to expect from you.

In a world full of uncertainties, being a consistent force can set you apart.

Patience

In the same way that you can't plant a seed today and expect a flower tomorrow, building connections and understanding requires time.

Cultivating patience involves:

- Recognising that deep connections don't form overnight.
- Giving people the space and time to open up, without pressure.
- Remaining calm, even when faced with challenges.

In the business of consulting, patience is often the key to unlocking deeper insights and relationships.

You might be thinking, *This sounds like a lot!* And yes, it can be. The beauty of the connection mindset is that it's not about being perfect; it's about making a genuine effort. You'll have days where you nail it and days where you could do better, and that's okay. What's important is that you're trying, learning, and growing.

As you cultivate connections, recognise that each person you meet is unique. They come with their own experiences, dreams and challenges. Welcome these differences, celebrate them.

Because it's through these diverse interactions that we truly enrich our own lives.

As we move forward in this step, we'll consider practical ways to strengthen these connections. For now, reflect on these mindsets. Consider which ones resonate most with you and which ones you might want to work on. Because with the right mindset, you're already halfway there.

***

MAPPING YOUR EXISTING NETWORK

Your professional network is more than just a collection of names. It's a dynamic web of relationships, each with the potential to unlock new business opportunities, collaborations or insights. In the Package Promote Scale Framework, each connection represents a valuable step towards the growth of your business.

Thanks to the digital era, managing and understanding this web has never been easier. Platforms such as LinkedIn and Facebook and Customer Relationship Management (CRMs) systems like ClickUp are invaluable for visualising, expanding and nurturing your network. Here's how you can leverage each:

- **LinkedIn**

  This platform lets you sort and engage with contacts, identifying thought leaders, decision-makers or potential collaborators. Through tags, notes, active participation in discussions and sharing content, you remain an active figure in your network.

  Tip: Always keep an eye on the 'People You May Know' feature – it's a goldmine for new connections.

- **Facebook**

  More than just social chatter, Facebook can be a hub for professional insights. As you become acquainted with industry peers, connecting on Facebook can prove valuable.

Professionals often share exclusive industry news, job leads and events here. Explore relevant groups, share your expertise and maintain a sense of professionalism, even in this more casual setting.

- **ClickUp (or other CRMs)**

    CRMs are your organisational backbone. They keep track of all your contacts, document interactions, remind you of follow-ups and help you categorise each connection. With them, you always stay in the loop.

Harnessing the power of these platforms allows you to:

- **Stay Close To Key Influencers**

    Regularly engage with industry leaders. Consider virtual meets or simply engage with their online content to foster a stronger relationship.

- **Identify Potential Collaborators**

    Be alert to synergy opportunities. A post or discussion on any platform can be the start of a promising partnership.

- **Spot And Fill Gaps In Your Network**

    Continually seek to expand and refine your connections. Set goals for new relationships and measure your growth periodically.

With an understanding of your current network and these tools at your disposal, you're not just networking, you're strategically positioning yourself for success. Up next, we'll explore strategies to further cultivate and enrich these connections.

***

REACHING OUT FOR GENUINE CONNECTION

Connecting with someone new on your favourite social media platform can be thrilling. It's like discovering a fresh connection in the digital world. While our ways of building relationships have evolved from face-to-face meetings to online interactions, the essence remains the same – taking the initiative to engage, make new friends, and explore different perspectives. Even though instant messaging and social media make communication quick and easy, reaching out to someone new can still feel daunting. Yet, it's a vital step for personal and professional growth. Embracing this can unlock new opportunities and enrich our lives with diverse perspectives.

Starting the conversation is more than just saying, 'Hi!' or sending generic text that reads, 'I'd like to add you to my professional network.' It's an art, one that requires thought, authenticity and a genuine interest in the person at the other end. Let's break this down into bite-size pieces.

First, before you even click that 'Message' button, take a moment. Put yourself in the other person's shoes. Would you appreciate an out-of-the-blue message? Perhaps not. However, if that message conveyed genuine interest, authenticity, and patience, it suddenly feels more inviting. So, here's what to do:

- **Start With A Genuine Introduction**

  Mention what drew you to their profile or their work. Maybe you read an insightful article they posted or you admire the company they're associated with. Being specific shows you've done your homework.

- **State Your Intentions Clearly**

  If you're seeking advice, say so. If you wish to collaborate or explore potential opportunities, mention that. Dancing around the topic can be off-putting.

- **Add A Personal Touch**

  Chat about a shared interest, maybe an industry event you both attended or a common connection. It makes the message warm and breaks the ice faster.

It's essential to be yourself. Authenticity shines through and people can often tell when someone is being insincere. It's like those handcrafted gifts you made as a kid, flawed but full of heart. Your message doesn't need to be perfect, but it needs to be genuinely you.

Listening, as you might already know, is crucial. And while you can't listen in the traditional sense when sending a message, you can certainly show that you're prepared to. By acknowledging the recipient's work, accomplishments or even challenges, you demonstrate empathy and understanding.

The tools at your disposal, like LinkedIn, Facebook or your trusty CRM, can be beneficial here. They're not just for keeping tabs on contacts but can be used actively in reaching out.

- On LinkedIn, engaging with posts or joining group discussions can serve as an informal introduction before you send a direct message.
- Facebook, with its relaxed environment, allows for a slightly more casual interaction, but you still need to maintain a respectable degree of professionalism.
- Your CRM can remind you to send that follow-up or even store templates of messages that have had high response rates in the past.

One more thing: when you do get a response, acknowledge it promptly. A thank you goes a long way and shows that you value the time they took to reply. As conversations progress, keep your interactions fluid. Allow the relationship to evolve organically. Not every connection will lead to a business opportunity. The goal is to build a rich, diverse network where relationships are based on mutual respect and understanding.

Reaching out is a skill that develops over time through practice. At its core, it's rooted in the basics of human interaction—kindness, authenticity and a genuine interest in understanding another person. As you start forging new connections, keep these principles close to your heart.

SEEING THINGS FROM THEIR PERSPECTIVE

Everyone likes to be heard and understood. There's comfort in knowing that someone is genuinely interested in us, our stories, and our aspirations. As a consultant, it's tempting to step into conversations eager to showcase your expertise or promote your services. However, real, lasting connections stem from turning the spotlight away from yourself and onto the other person. Why? Because when people feel seen and heard, a bridge of trust and likability begins to form. For consultants, this bridge is crucial. It's the foundation upon which strong professional relationships are built. Such relationships not only enhance personal growth but make it considerably smoother to leverage and promote one's services package in line with the Package Promote Scale Framework.

Think back to those conversations where you genuinely felt the person you were speaking to was fully invested in understanding you. How did it make you feel? Valued? Important? Comfortable? That's precisely the feeling to aim for when interacting with individuals in your professional network. By making your engagements about them, you show that you care enough to grasp their perspective, fostering an environment where they feel acknowledged and accepted.

This transition from focusing on oneself to emphasising the other person's viewpoint isn't just a strategy; it's a mindset shift. Let's investigate how you can foster this shift and why it's invaluable in your consulting business.

This shift from focusing on yourself to really seeing things from the other person's perspective isn't just a strategy; it involves a different mindset. Here's how you can encourage this shift and why it's so valuable in your consulting business.

Imagine you're reaching out to someone. Maybe you've crafted the perfect message, mentioned all the right things and hit send. Then the wait begins. Days turn into weeks and there's no reply.

It's easy to jump to conclusions: *Did I say something wrong? Are they not interested? Maybe they don't see the potential collaboration the way I do.* While all these thoughts are natural, it's essential to pause for a moment and see things from their perspective.

When you understand another person's viewpoint, your approach shifts. It's no longer about what you want but about finding a common ground. And how do you do that? It starts with genuine interest. When you're curious about their work, their challenges and their aspirations, you're showing that you care. Your interactions change from being transactional to relational.

Pair this interest with empathy. Suppose you've noticed someone working on a particularly challenging project or sharing something personal on a social platform. Acknowledging their situation and offering words of encouragement or support demonstrates empathy. By doing so, you show that you see them as more than just a professional contact – you recognise them as a human being with feelings, emotions, and challenges like everyone else.

This is where authenticity comes in. People can often sense when interactions are forced or fake. When you're genuinely trying to understand their perspective, the conversation flows better. There's a natural rhythm to it. You're not trying to impress or say the right things, you're simply being you.

Of course, understanding another's perspective requires patience. Not everyone will open up immediately, and not every interaction will lead to instant results. Sometimes, it's about planting the seed and nurturing the relationship over time.

Using tools like LinkedIn or Facebook can also give you insights into someone's professional background and personal interests. Engage with their posts, understand their line of work and see the kind of content they resonate with. It's not about stalking but about understanding them better. If you're using a CRM like

ClickUp, jot down these insights so you have a clearer picture the next time you interact with them.

Here are a few tips to help you see things from their perspective:

- **Acknowledge Their Work**

  Recognising someone's achievements or milestones shows that you've been paying attention. It's a small gesture but carries a lot of weight.

- **Ask Open-Ended Questions**

  Instead of leading the conversation, let them share their stories and thoughts. You'll be surprised how much you can learn by just listening.

- **Be Respectful Of Their Time**

  We all have our schedules. If someone can't chat right away or needs to reschedule a call, be understanding. Remember, patience is a virtue.

- **Celebrate Their Successes**

  If they've achieved something noteworthy, celebrate with them. It could be as simple as leaving a congratulatory comment or sending a quick message.

In the end, seeing things from another's perspective is about building trust. It's about understanding that every individual is unique and has their own set of challenges and dreams. Tapping into these not only makes a connection but also builds a bond. And as you continue to foster these bonds, your professional network becomes a web of genuine relationships, each with its own story and potential.

***

COMMUNICATING EFFECTIVELY

Effective communication is a key part of being a consultant or, really, being good at any job where you deal with people. It's like the glue that holds all your interactions together. And here's the thing: it's not what you say or how much you know but about making sure that the person you're talking to gets your message, loud and clear, and feels respected in the process.

So, what are some effective communication techniques?

For starters, active listening. This means really focusing on the person speaking, rather than waiting for your turn to talk. You might be surprised at how much better you understand someone when you truly listen. And they can tell when you're really with them, which makes them feel important.

Next up is clarity. Whether you're explaining a complicated concept or laying out your consulting services, keep your language simple. You want the person you're talking to nodding along because they get it, not because they're lost but too embarrassed to say so.

And while we're at it, don't forget the power of questions. Asking questions does a couple of awesome things. It helps you get a clearer picture of what the other person is thinking or needing and it shows them that you're invested in the conversation. It's like saying, 'I want to understand you better.'

Consider your tone of voice. The way you say something can totally change the message. A warm, friendly tone can make all the difference in how your words are received. It can be the difference between someone feeling at ease or on edge.

Let's consider your body language, too. Your posture, eye contact and gestures need to all say, *I'm open and friendly*. It's amazing how a simple smile or nod can make people feel at ease.

Here's a list of handy pointers that can really strengthen your communication:

- **Active Engagement**

  Whenever you're in a conversation, be all in. Listen actively, showing genuine interest in what's being said. This not only demonstrates your respect for the other person but also makes it easier to find common ground.

- **Clarity Over Complexity**

  Keep things simple. Your aim is to be understood, not to impress with big words or complex explanations. Being clear invites others to engage openly with you without feeling overwhelmed or intimidated.

- **Inquisitiveness**

  Curiosity fosters connections. Ask questions to go deeper into what someone is sharing with you. It not only helps in gathering more information but also shows that you're keen to understand them better.

- **Reliability**

  It's crucial that your actions match your words. When you say you'll do something, such as, 'I'll follow that up on Tuesday', make a point of delivering on that commitment. This forms a solid foundation for trust and credibility.

- **Empathetic Approach**

  Always be mindful of the feelings and emotions of the other person. An understanding nod, a compassionate response or simply acknowledging someone's feelings can go a long way in strengthening your bond.

- **Relaxed Posture**

  Even without words, we're always communicating. Maintain a relaxed posture that communicates ease and comfort. Make eye contact and use gestures that show you're at ease. It's a nonverbal way of saying, *I'm here with you in a comfortable and genuine manner.*

- **Feedback Loop**

  After sharing information or an idea, always check if the person you're communicating with is on the same page. This not only ensures clarity but also gives them an opportunity to voice any concerns or offer feedback.

As a consultant, your goal is to not only share your knowledge but to create a connection that makes your clients or colleagues feel valued and understood. Good communication is about being heard and understanding others. Keep these techniques in mind and you'll be on your way to sharing your message and making sure it resonates with those who hear it.

***

RECOGNISING WHEN THERE ISN'T A FIT

You're in a meeting room, face-to-face with a potential client. Everything started off great. The energy was palpable, the initial discussions seemed productive, and you both seemed eager to get started. However, as the talks progress, a nagging feeling creeps in. It begins to dawn on you that you and this client might not be singing from the same songbook. Your goals, approach or even values appear to be drifting apart. Do you push forward in hopes that things will iron out or do you acknowledge the disconnect?

It's a reality many consultants face: not every client or project will be the right fit. While it's paramount to build and sustain client relationships, it's equally essential to recognise when the alignment isn't there. After all, entering into a partnership where both parties aren't fully in sync can lead to miscommunications, unmet expectations and, in some cases, strained professional ties.

Identifying these mismatches early on and managing them with tact is key. With understanding and respect at the forefront, even if you decide not to take on a project or client, the relationship remains intact and future opportunities remain open.

So, let's explore how to discern these situations and approach them with professionalism.

The trick is to detect these mismatches early on and handle them well. When there's respect and understanding, even a 'no' can pave the way for future possibilities.

What are the telltale signs? Here are five to lookout for:

- **Difference In Values, Principles Or Expectations**

  If you're dedicated to inclusivity in your projects but you find that your potential client is not prioritising diverse stakeholder voices, it can become a point of contention. Aligning with people and organisations that share your values is not just about feeling good; it's about ensuring long-term collaboration and growth.

- **Communication Barriers**

  We all have our own communication styles, but if you're continually misinterpreting each other or feeling that things are left unsaid, it might be an indication of a deeper mismatch.

- **Misaligned Goals And Priorities**

  If you find that your objectives for the project or collaboration don't align with those of your potential client or partner, it could lead to friction down the road. For instance, if you're focused on creating a sustainable, long-term solution but your client is only interested in quick, short-term gains, it might be challenging to find common ground.

- **Lack of Respect For Expertise**

  If you feel that your potential client or collaborator doesn't value or respect your expertise and insights, it could be a red flag. This might manifest as them constantly questioning your recommendations, ignoring your advice or undermining your authority in your area of specialisation. A healthy partnership needs to be built on mutual trust and respect for each other's expertise.

- **Incompatible Working Styles**

  Everyone has their preferred way of working, but if your working styles are drastically different, it could lead to conflicts and inefficiencies. For example, if you thrive on structure and clear deadlines but your potential collaborator prefers a more relaxed, go-with-the-flow approach, it might be difficult to get in sync and make progress together.

How do you approach these situations with grace? Here are some handy pointers to guide you:

- **Trust Your Instincts**

  Often, your gut feeling is your best guide. If something feels off, take a step back and evaluate. It doesn't mean making impulsive decisions but rather taking a moment to reflect on your feelings.

- **Open A Dialogue**

  Before making any decisions, have an honest conversation. Discuss your reservations, listen to theirs and see if there's a middle ground. Keep in mind that communication is a two-way street.

- **Stay Respectful**

  Even if you decide not to proceed with deepening a connection or an engagement, always part ways with respect. Express gratitude for their time and leave the door open for future interactions.

- **Seek Feedback**

  Sometimes, it's beneficial to ask for feedback. Perhaps there's something you can improve on or maybe they have insights that can benefit you in the long run.

- **Reflect And Learn**

  Every interaction, even when it doesn't lead to a paid engagement, is an opportunity to learn. Reflect on what worked and what didn't, and then focus on how you can improve in the future.

Recognising when there isn't a fit is not a failure; it's an exercise in self-awareness and discernment. And while it might be tempting to push forward in the hopes that things might change, it's important to realise when to let go. Letting go can often open space for new, more aligned opportunities to come your way.

What if you're on the receiving end? What if someone else feels there isn't a fit? It's natural to feel a bit disappointed or even hurt. Handling such situations with grace is crucial. Thank them for their honesty, ask for feedback and recognise that every no is a step closer to a yes that truly aligns with your goals and values.

Of course, while much of our focus has been on client–consultant relationships, it's essential to note that these principles aren't confined solely to this dynamic. When dealing with collaborators, partners and even subcontractors, similar challenges and decisions might arise. Maybe you're considering a partnership with a fellow consultant for a project or thinking of bringing a subcontractor on board to help with a particular task. The same red flags, like misaligned values or communication challenges, can pop up. Much like with clients, it's essential to trust your instincts here. If something feels amiss or you're having second thoughts, it's always a wise move to step back and reassess the relationship. After all, these relationships also play a pivotal role in the success and smooth progression of your work. Ensuring you're on solid ground with partners and collaborators is just as crucial as establishing a harmonious bond with clients.

Recognising when there's a fit and when there isn't, and handling these situations with understanding and respect, paves the way for genuine, lasting, and rewarding connections. It's not about the quantity of your connections but the quality.

And sometimes, quality means knowing when to say yes and when to respectfully say no.

***

CONCLUSION

Now is a good time to take a few moments to reflect on, absorb and appreciate the intricacies of our relationships. If there's one takeaway that stands tall, it's this: in creating meaningful connections, it's truly the little things that count. While grand gestures make headlines, trust, respect and mutual growth are often built by the consistent, seemingly insignificant actions we engage in daily.

Imagine a vast tapestry, rich in colours, patterns and textures. Each conversation you have, every meeting you attend and every email you send forms a single thread in this magnificent artwork. Over time, these threads intertwine, representing what's at the heart of your professional relationships. They come together to create a strong, vibrant and resilient network. And much like this tapestry, the true beauty of our professional world lies in its diversity – the myriad of people we encounter, the broad spectrum of discussions we engage in and the varied viewpoints we consider and adopt.

Here are some of the key elements that make your professional network unique and valuable:

- **Daily Dedication**

  The significance of your presence isn't captured in grand events or milestone celebrations but in the everyday commitment you bring to the table. It's like the consistent care a gardener provides, helping a plant thrive through regular nurturing, rather than with a sudden deluge. This includes genuinely listening to others, honouring commitments and being transparent when things don't go as planned.

- **Being The Rock**

  Your reliability can provide stability for others who find themselves in more challenging circumstances. Consistently offering insight, support, and assistance makes you a reliable figure others can turn to, solidifying your bonds and fortifying trust.

- **Celebrating Together**

  Those little moments of joy when someone recognises your effort or shares in your happiness are truly special. Such simple gestures of appreciation and the collective celebration of small wins breathe life and warmth into professional connections.

- **Making Every Interaction Count**

  The fleeting chat with a new someone at an event, the acknowledgment of a collaborator's work, the brainstorming session with a client – each of these encounters holds the potential for deeper connection.

- **Creating A Welcoming Environment**

  Building connections is like tending a garden. While sowing seeds is essential, it's equally vital to foster an environment conducive to growth. This involves welcoming different perspectives, fostering an environment of mutual learning, and appreciating our collective progress.

The heart and soul of our engagements lie in their authenticity. It's not merely about being physically present in a conversation but wholly immersing ourselves. It's about valuing the person across the table, understanding their perspective and collaborating for shared success. Each interaction becomes a dance of mutual respect, understanding and reciprocity, laying the foundation for a connection that's both meaningful and enduring.

Your value and the esteem others within your network hold for you isn't defined by occasional grand feats. It's reflected in the daily acts of professionalism, kindness and genuine engagement. Consistently offering the best version of yourself enriches your own professional growth and enhances your interactions with those around you.

Cherish the tapestry of relationships you've woven and continue to weave. Each thread, no matter how thin or brief, contributes to the grand design. Value them, nurture them and watch as they come together to create a masterpiece of connections that are as enduring as they are beautiful.

***

CASE STUDY

Melanie, a fundraising consultant for educational institutions, had extensive knowledge in her field and a record of success in helping her clients achieve their goals. However, despite her expertise, Melanie struggled to build a strong network of connections within her industry.

One of the challenges Melanie faced was initiating meaningful conversations at networking events and conferences. She regularly found herself stuck in surface-level small talk, failing to establish genuine connections with potential clients or collaborators.

Another challenge for Melanie was following up after meeting someone new. Melanie collected business cards and made promises to stay in touch, but often failed to follow through, allowing potentially mutually beneficial relationships to slip through her fingers.

Recognising the importance of a strong professional network, Melanie decided to take a more strategic approach to building connections.

First, Melanie set clear goals for each networking event she attended. Rather than aiming to collect as many business cards as possible, she focused on having meaningful conversations with a few key people. She researched attendees beforehand and prepared thoughtful questions to initiate conversations.

At the events, Melanie made a point to listen actively and show genuine interest in the people she met. She asked about their challenges, goals and recent successes, looking for ways to offer insights or support. When Melanie did talk about her own work, she was careful to share stories and examples that focused on the client, not on herself.

To ensure she followed up effectively, Melanie set aside dedicated time after each event to review the connections she'd made. For each person she wanted to build a relationship with, she drafted a personalised email within 24 hours of the event. In these emails, Melanie referenced specific points from their conversation, shared a relevant article or resource and expressed her desire to stay in touch.

Melanie also made a point to connect with her new contacts on LinkedIn. In addition to sending a personalised connection request, she engaged with an item of their content by liking or sharing it within her own network. This helped to keep Melanie top of mind with the contacts and demonstrate her ongoing interest in their work.

For particularly promising connections, Melanie suggested a follow-up call or coffee meeting. She approached these not as sales pitches but as opportunities to learn more about their work and explore potential ways to support each other.

Being strategic and intentional in her networking efforts allowed Melanie to see a significant shift in the quality and depth of her professional relationships. Her genuine approach and consistent follow-through helped her stand out and build trust with potential clients and partners.

Over time, Melanie's network became a powerful asset. She was the first consultant people thought of when asked for referrals and partnership opportunities and had a wide circle of colleagues to learn from and collaborate with. Focusing on creating value and engaging consistently allowed Melanie to grow her list of contacts into a thriving network of meaningful connections.

***

Lessons Learned

Here are the key takeaways from Melanie's path to personal growth:

- **Set Intentional Networking Goals**

  Rather than aiming for quantity, focus on having meaningful conversations with a few key individuals at each event.

- **Listen Actively And Show Genuine Interest**

  Ask thoughtful questions and look for ways to offer insights or support based on what you learn.

- **Share Stories That Demonstrate Your Value**

  When discussing your own work, focus on examples that showcase your expertise and the impact you've had for clients.

- **Follow Up Promptly And Personally**

  Send a personalised email within 24 hours of meeting someone, referencing specific points from your conversation.

- **Engage On LinkedIn**

  Connect with new contacts on LinkedIn and engage with their content to stay top of mind.

- **Suggest Follow-Up Conversations**

  For particularly promising connections, suggest a call or coffee meeting to learn more about their work and explore collaboration opportunities.

- **Focus On Creating Value**

  Rather than seeking personal gain, approach networking with a mindset of enriching others.

Applying these lessons and being strategic in your networking efforts enables you to build robust, high-quality professional networks that support your business goals and provide a greater degree of professional and personal satisfaction.

***

ACTION STEPS

Building genuine connections is essential for growing your consulting business. Follow these action steps to develop meaningful relationships:

- Cultivate an entrepreneurial networking mindset.
- Schedule and manage daily networking activities.
- Be proactive in nurturing relationships.
- Assess and adjust your networking approach regularly.
- Align your networking decisions with your values and vision.
- Embrace networking challenges with curiosity and determination.

Ready to go deeper? Download the free bonus collection at: www.packagepromotescale.com/bonus

Step 6 – Nurture

When you think about the word 'nurture,' what comes to mind? Maybe it's the careful way a gardener tends to their plants or how a teacher patiently helps students understand a tricky concept. In our lives, nurturing is the gentle art of helping something or someone grow, providing support and creating an environment in which they can flourish.

In this step, we'll focus on nurturing relationships, especially the connections we make in our daily lives and careers.

Think about your best friend. What makes your bond with them special? Is it because they've got your back, or is it because you've shared so many laughs as well as a few tears? It's probably a mix of both, along with countless other little moments where you've both shown that you care about each other.

That's what nurturing is all about. It's being there, really being present, for others in the small moments just as much as the big ones. It's the check-in texts when you know they've got a lot on their plate or the high-fives when they land a new client. Nurturing in the professional world isn't so different to nurturing our friends. It's about creating strong, healthy and lasting connections.

Here's how you might do that:

- **Remember The Details**

  Did they mention a big weekend plan? On Monday, ask them how it went.

- **Listen More Than You Talk**

  Understand what's important to them.

- **Be a Cheerleader For Their Successes**

  Celebrate their wins with a word of congratulations.

- **Share Something Helpful**

  It could be advice, a contact or an interesting article.

- **Just Say Hello**

  Sometimes a quick message or postcard can make all the difference.

Nurturing doesn't mean you have to be best friends with everyone you meet in your career. It's more about building a network of people who you genuinely care about and who care about you too. It's about finding a balance between being professional and being human.

You might be wondering, *Why put in all this effort?* Well, consider a tree. If you plant it and walk away, it might grow but it might not be strong or healthy. If you water it, make sure it gets enough sun and protect it from harsh weather, that tree is much more likely to thrive. It's the same with relationships – the more you nurture them, the stronger and more rewarding they can become.

Turning to the practical, how can you nurture these relationships without feeling like you're spreading yourself too thin?

Here's a little guide:

- Make time in your schedule to reach out to people. It doesn't have to be long, even a few minutes can matter.

- Keep a list of who you've connected with and a couple of notes about what's important to them.
- Use tools such as calendar reminders to help you remember to check in.
- Help out when you can but be honest about what you're able to do.

Nurturing relationships is a two-way street. It's not just about what you can do for others but also what they can do for you. It's involves creating a circle of support where everyone feels valued and understood.

What about when things get busy? It's important to know how to say no or not right now in a way that's kind and respectful. You can't do everything for everyone all the time. Nurturing is about quality, not quantity.

Throughout your personal and professional development, you'll find that the relationships you've nurtured will become one of your greatest assets. These connections will be there to celebrate your successes and offer advice when you're facing challenges, and sometimes, they'll lead to opportunities that you never expected.

In the end, nurturing is about building a community – your community. It's the planting seeds of kindness and compassion and watching them grow into something beautiful.

***

NURTURING AND WHY YOU NEED TO DO IT

Why put effort into nurturing relationships? It sounds nice and all, but is it really that important? You bet it is, and here's why.

First up, think about the feeling you get when someone remembers your birthday without a Facebook reminder or when someone asks how an unwell family member is doing. It feels pretty great, right? That's because someone took the time to show they care about you. When we genuinely nurture our relationships, we're doing just that – showing people they matter.

Also, while nurturing relationships makes others feel good, it helps you out too. Nurturing can:

- **Build Trust**

  When people know you're there for them, they are more likely to trust you. That trust is like gold – hard to earn but incredibly valuable.

- **Open Doors**

  Ever heard the saying, 'it's not what you know, it's who you know?' Well, there's some truth to that. When you have a network of people who care about you, they might think of you when opportunities pop up.

- **Make The Hard Times Easier**

  Everyone hits a bump now and then. Having people to lean on during difficult periods can make those bumps feel a lot smaller.

- **Make You Feel Good**

  Yes, being kind and helpful makes you feel warm and fuzzy inside. And who doesn't want that?

So, how do you make nurturing a part of your everyday life? It's easier than you might think:

- Make it a habit to ask people how they're doing and really listen to their answers.
- When someone tells you about something big coming up in their life, jot it down and ask them about it later.
- If you see an article or a video that reminds you of a conversation you had with someone, send it their way.
- Share your thoughts and insights and be authentic.
- Author and inspirational speaker Simon Sinek said, 'People

don't buy what you do, they buy why you do it.' Share your origin/founder story and your 'big why'.

Nurturing relationships does not equate to keeping score. You're not doing nice things for others just so they'll do nice things for you. It's about genuinely wanting to be there for the people in your life. When you do that, you'll find they will want to be there for you too.

Sometimes, you might feel like you're too busy to nurture your relationships. Here's the deal: everyone's busy. But it's the little things that often make the biggest difference. A quick text or a 5-minute call can mean the world to someone. You don't need to carve out huge chunks of your day; just make the time you do spend count.

Lastly, let's not forget that you're part of this equation too. Nurturing relationships means taking care of yourself as well. You've got to put on your own oxygen mask first, right? Make sure you're looking after your health, setting aside time for things you love and reaching out for support when you need it.

***

NURTURING A PROFESSIONAL RELATIONSHIP

Building strong relationships is like having a secret superpower. It's not like being able to lift a car or fly, but it sure can help you forge ahead in business. So, how exactly do you nurture your professional relationships?

Here are some straightforward ways to make those connections grow strong and healthy:

- **Show Up And Speak Up**

  Just like you can't make friends if you never leave your house, you can't build relationships if you don't put yourself out there. Get involved in meetings and discussions. When you're part of a conversation, you become someone who people know they can talk to.

- **Listen Well**

  Ever had someone tune you out? It's not fun. In business, listening to others is super important. It shows that you respect what they have to say which makes them feel valued.

- **Do What You Say You'll Do**

  If you tell someone you'll send them some information by Friday, make sure you do it. Keeping your word is a big deal. It builds trust, and trust is like the glue in relationships – it holds everything together.

- **Be Helpful**

  This doesn't mean doing other people's jobs for them. It's more like when someone is trying to reach something high up and you offer them a ladder. In the office, it could be as simple as sharing a helpful article or giving a bit of advice if asked.

- **Take A Stand**

  Share causes and issues you care about and support others in theirs.

- **Stay Positive**

  We all have bad days but nobody likes a constant complainer or gossip. Keeping a positive attitude, even when things are tough, makes you someone people want to be around.

- **Be A Cheerleader**

  And no, this doesn't mean bringing pompoms to work. It's about cheering on your colleagues when they do well. A simple message saying, 'Great job!' can go a long way.

- **Keep In Touch**

  You don't need to message your work friends every day but checking in now and then keeps the relationship alive. A quick email or a chat over coffee will do the trick.

When it comes to nurturing professional relationships, there's no room for being fake or just trying to get ahead. People can usually tell if you're not being genuine, and that's no good. It's about truly caring about the individuals you work with and wanting everyone to succeed.

So, you're doing all these things, being involved, listening, keeping promises, helping out, staying upbeat, cheering on your colleagues and remaining in touch. What else could you be doing? Well, there are several things to keep an eye on:

- **Respecting Boundaries**

  Just like you wouldn't call a new friend in the middle of the night to ask what they're up to, you must respect people's personal space and time in business too.

- **Balancing Give and Take**

  Relationships need to be balanced equally. If you're always asking for favours or referrals and never helping others, that's not going to work out well. Make sure to give back as much as you get.

- **Being Patient**

  Good relationships don't happen overnight. They take time to build, just like it takes time to learn to play an instrument or master a video game. Don't rush it. Let things grow naturally.

- **Staying Open To Learning**

  Be curious to learn about different industries, methodologies and approaches. Be willing to learn from others, no matter their role. Everyone has something valuable to share.

While this might seem like a lot to do, it's not that different from being a good friend or teammate. It's about treating people the way you'd like to be treated, with kindness, respect and a bit of cheerleading when it's needed. Sometimes nurturing relationships can be met with suspicion, as though you may have ulterior motives. The key is to not have any expectations or be attached to the outcomes or result. Just be you. Everyone else is taken.

As you move forward in your career, keep these tips in mind. They might seem small but they're mighty. Nurturing your professional relationships sets you up for a world of opportunities, support, and even fun. And that's something worth investing in, don't you think?

***

TRANSITIONING FROM CONNECTION TO CLIENT

To transform a professional connection into a client, begin by understanding them: who they are, what their business struggles with and what they aim to achieve.

Here's how you can foster that connection effectively:

- Take the time to really understand their business needs by engaging in meaningful conversations.
- Show genuine interest in their challenges, rather than seeing them only as potential revenue.
- Keep your commitments and promises realistic. If you can't do something, it's better to be transparent about it.
- Share your stories of helping others but focus on the relevance to their situation so it doesn't come off as self-promotion.
- Be consistent in your communication. Quick responses and availability go a long way in showing that you're reliable.
- Ask targeted questions to deepen your understanding of their needs and demonstrate your investment in their success.
- Offer insights or advice that may help them, giving them a glimpse of the value you could bring to their business.
- Understand that good things take time and be patient as the relationship matures into a business opportunity.

When the time feels right to discuss the possibility of working together, consider these approaches:

- During a catch up or casual conversation, gently steer the topic towards how you could help them with a challenge they've mentioned. Another, less direct, way is to share a story about someone that you helped who had the same challenge.
- If you sense that they're open to it, don't shy away from being direct. Propose a meeting or call to discuss a potential collaboration in detail.
- Position yourself as a helper, not a salesperson. Extend an offer of help on a specific issue they are facing, suggesting a time when you could contribute your expertise.

The transition from connection to client needs to feel natural. It's important for the potential client to feel they are making the choice to engage your services because they value what you offer, not because they're being pushed into a decision. Think about how you make choices every day. You opt for things because you see their benefit, not because someone tells you to choose them.

It's perfectly normal if not every connection turns into a client. Like any other aspect of life, not every interaction is destined to become a deeper relationship. It's all about finding the right match. When you do find it, and you will, it can lead to a mutually beneficial partnership that can have a lasting impact.

Keep these guidelines in mind as you go about cultivating your business connections. With patience, authenticity and consistent effort, you'll be in an excellent position to see some of those connections make the exciting leap to becoming clients.

***

BEING THERE FOR THE LONG HAUL

Building lasting relationships in business is all about consistent effort and reliability. When you first start working with a client, you're both getting to know each other, figuring out how to communicate effectively and setting the foundation for a potentially long-term partnership. Maintaining that relationship requires the same level of care and attention you put in at the very beginning – day in and day out, project after project.

You've probably heard that first impressions are important, and they are, but what really matters in the professional world is every impression you make after that. It's about proving that you can be trusted to deliver consistently over time. Your goal is to become the trusted expert your clients instinctively contact when they need your specific skills.

As discussed earlier, nurturing relationships is key to success in any context. When it comes to maintaining long-term client relationships, many of the same principles apply but with a specific focus on delivering continuous value. Here's how you can achieve this:

- **Staying Connected**

  Regular communication is key. This doesn't mean sending emails every day but rather reaching out with purpose. When you come across information that could benefit your client, share it with them. It shows that you're thinking about their needs even when you're not on the clock.

- **Being a Good Listener**

  Whenever you're communicating with your client, really listen to what they're saying. This not only helps you understand their needs better but also shows that you respect their perspective. Recalling the details of your last conversation and following up on them can make your client feel heard and valued.

- **Remaining Informed**

  Keeping updated on what's happening in their industry allows you to offer insights they might not have come across themselves. This proactive approach can help you spot opportunities for your client and demonstrates your commitment to their success.

- **Celebrating Their Successes**

  When your client achieves something, whether it's hitting a target or earning recognition, acknowledge it. A simple message congratulating them can strengthen your relationship and show that you care and are invested in their success.

- **Building Trust With Transparency**

  Always be honest with your client, especially if you encounter challenges. If a problem arises, communicate it promptly and clearly, along with any potential solutions you might have. This honesty helps to build a foundation of trust and is critical for a lasting business relationship.

Consistently demonstrating your commitment to your clients' success can transform a typical consultant–client relationship into a deep, enduring partnership. This shift in dynamic opens the door to long-term engagements, repeat business and exciting new growth opportunities. Nurturing client relationships creates a win-win scenario, where clients benefit from your ongoing support and expertise and your business thrives on a foundation of loyal, satisfied clients.

***

DEALING WITH DIFFICULT SITUATIONS

When you're working with people, it's pretty much a given that not everything will go smoothly all the time. Just like in any other area of life, you're going to run into tough situations sometimes. These bumps in the road can feel a little scary but they're opportunities to show just what you're made of. Handling these tricky moments with care and skill can make your professional relationships even stronger.

Imagine a project you're working on hits a snag. Maybe something has taken longer than expected or there's been a mix-up with the information you've been given. It's not the end of the world but it sure can feel like it when you're in the thick of things.

Here's what you can do:

- **Keep Cool**

  The first step is to stay calm. If you're upset or worried, it's going to be harder to think clearly. Take a deep breath and recognise that every problem has a solution.

- **Talk It Out**

  Once you're feeling steady, it's time to talk to your client. Be honest and straightforward about what's going on. It's important to keep that line of communication open.

- **Apologise If Needed**

  If the difficult situation was due to a mistake on your part, don't be afraid to say you're sorry. Owning up to errors is a big part of building trust.

- **Listen Carefully**

  After you've explained the situation, give your client a chance to talk. Listen to their concerns and understand where they're coming from. This can help you figure out the best way to move forward.

- **Work On A Solution**

  This is where you put on your thinking cap and get to work. Come up with a plan to set things right. It might involve a little extra time or resources, but finding a way to solve the problem is crucial.

- **Follow Through**

  Once you've got a plan, you need to make it happen. Do what you've said you're going to do. This shows your client that they can count on you, even when things get tough.

- **Learn From The Experience**

  After the situation has been handled, take some time to think about what happened. What can you learn from this? How can you avoid similar problems in the future?

- **Check Back In**

  Even after the issue is resolved, check back in with your client. Make sure they're happy with how things were handled and see if there's anything else you can do for them.

Difficult situations aren't fun but they don't have to be disasters either. Dealing with problems head-on, communicating clearly, and showing that you're committed to making things right can turn a tough situation into a display of your professionalism and dedication. Plus, each challenge you overcome not only makes you a better consultant but also deepens the trust between you and your client. And in the world of business, trust is like gold.

***

LEARNING TO NURTURE YOURSELF

As a busy consultant, it's easy to get caught up in the needs of clients and forget about the person who's meeting those needs – *you*. It's like the chef who is always cooking gourmet meals for others but doesn't nourish themselves properly. Eventually, they won't have the energy to get through the day. That's why it is super important to learn how to take care of yourself. This doesn't have anything to do with being selfish but is about keeping yourself in top shape and, as such, being able to do your best for others. So, how do you nurture yourself in a busy world? Let's break it down.

First off, think about the basics of self-care. These are the things that keep you running at full speed:

- **Getting Enough Sleep**

  This one's huge. Sleep is like charging your body's batteries.

Without enough of it, everything else gets harder.

- **Eating Right**

  Food is fuel. Eating a bunch of junk food is like putting low-grade gas in a sports car. You want to make sure you're getting plenty of good stuff like fruits, veggies and whole grains.

- **Staying Active**

  Your body is built to move. Exercise isn't just for athletes; everyone can benefit from moving their body. It helps to clear your mind and boosts your mood.

- **Taking Breaks**

  Ever tried to keep reading when your eyes are tired? Doesn't work too well, does it? The same goes for working nonstop. You need short breaks to keep your mind fresh.

Next up, think about how you handle stress. Stress is like a heavy backpack; the longer you carry it, the heavier it feels. Learning to manage stress is key:

- **Find Relaxing Activities**

  Do things that help you unwind. This could be drawing, playing music or just chilling with your favourite book or show.

- **Talk About It**

  Sharing what's on your mind can lighten that stress load. Chat with a friend, family member or counsellor.

- **Practise Mindfulness**

  This can be as simple as taking some deep breaths or meditating. It's about being in the moment and giving your brain a break from the hustle.

- **Stay Organised**

  A messy schedule can be a big source of stress. Keep track of your tasks and plan your time. Knowing what you need to do and when you need to do it can give you a sense of control.

Don't forget about the fun stuff. All work and no play isn't just boring; it can lead to burnout. Make time for the things you love:

- **Pursue Hobbies and Interests**

  Whether it's collecting stamps or hiking, make time for your hobbies. They're part of what makes you *you*.

- **Socialise**

  Hang out with people who make you laugh and feel good. Friends and family can be a great source of energy and inspiration.

- **Laugh**

  It might be an old saying, but laughter really can be the best medicine. It relaxes you and makes life more fun.

Lastly, nurturing yourself isn't a one-time deal. It's a daily practice. Keep an eye on how you're feeling and what you need. Maybe one day you need a little more rest and another day you need some extra time with friends. It's all about listening to yourself and responding with kindness.

Taking care of yourself not only does a favour for your future self but also sets a good example for those around you. Just like the safety instructions on a plane which advise you to put on your own oxygen mask before helping others, you can offer way more help when you're at your best.

So, go ahead, make self-care a priority. Be the best you can be – for you and for everyone who counts on you.

***

CONCLUSION

In closing out this step, recognise that every interaction you have, each piece of advice you share and every problem you solve adds up. They aren't just isolated moments; they're steps on a path leading you to become a better version of yourself and a standout professional.

Some of these steps may seem small, such as making sure you're really listening to someone's ideas, sending a quick note to check in on a client or even taking an extra five minutes to make sure your work is just right. Just like drops in a bucket, these actions fill up and eventually overflow, demonstrating the depth of your care and commitment.

We've talked about a lot of things in this step:

- **Being Present**

  It's all about showing up fully, ready to engage and contribute.

- **Consistent Effort**

  It is not grand gestures but the everyday dedication to doing good work that really counts.

- **Adaptability**

  Being flexible and open to change helps you grow and helps those around you feel supported through the ups and downs.

- **Communication**

  Clear, honest and kind words can bridge gaps and build strong foundations.

- **Respect**

  Valuing others, including their time and their ideas, goes a long way in forming lasting bonds.

- **Encouragement**

  Recognising the hard work and successes of others can turn

a good team into a great one.

- **Growth Mindset**

    Keeping your mind open to learning not only helps you but also encourages others to keep growing too.

It's not just about what you achieve daily; it's about who you are while doing it. Are you kind? Are you patient? Are you giving each task your best shot? These are the qualities that people remember. They are the things that make you someone others love to work with and that build up a reputation you can be proud of.

Don't lose sight of these small yet significant actions. Even when days get busy or challenges pop up, these are the habits that will help you stay on track, making every day a little bit better than the last.

And please take care of yourself. Like watering a plant or saving for a big goal, it's the regular, thoughtful care that keeps you at your best. You're at the heart of all you do, so give yourself the kindness and support you offer so readily to others.

***

CASE STUDY

Adam is a dedicated capacity-building consultant who works with volunteer committees and boards. He aimed to solidify his network by being a continuous source of value to his peers.

Adam's situation underscores what can happen when we neglect to nurture our network of connections. He generally didn't reach out to his network, and when he did it was somewhat out of the blue. Adam tried sending mass emails to his list of over 200 current and former clients. He gave social media a go by sharing updates about what he was up to in his business. He even attended a few networking events. Unfortunately, none of these activities created the relationships Adam was aiming for, and his approach led to minimal engagement and a lack of deep connections. His efforts simply didn't resonate with what was essential for real impact. Without a consistent approach, Adam's attempts were often forgotten, and the potential for meaningful and enduring relationships was lost.

One specific challenge Adam faced was maintaining regular contact with his network. He found himself getting caught up in day-to-day tasks and letting valuable opportunities slip through the cracks. Another issue was the generic nature of his outreach. His mass emails and social media posts lacked the personalisation needed to truly engage his ideal clients.

Recognising the need for change, Adam committed to a more thoughtful and consistent approach. He started by segmenting his network based on their interests and needs. This allowed him to tailor his outreach and provide more relevant value to each group.

Next, Adam set aside dedicated time each week for nurturing his relationships. He scheduled reminders to reach out to people and offered out-of-hours catch ups to make it more convenient for them. He made a point of congratulating people on their successes, shared relevant articles and resources and offered introductions when he saw an opportunity for benefit between the parties (even if it didn't benefit him directly).

To keep his outreach personal, Adam sent individual emails and messages. He referenced specific conversations or shared experiences, showing that he was truly paying attention and cared about the relationship. He also tried to meet with people in person, when possible, even if just for a quick coffee chat.

Adam also started sharing more of his own journey and insights. He wrote thoughtful blog posts and articles that showcased his expertise while also revealing his challenges and learnings. This vulnerability helped him connect with his network on a deeper level.

The impact of these changes made a world of difference. Adam's network started to see him as a genuine, reliable partner and an advocate for their own success. They were more responsive to his outreach and more likely to think of him when opportunities arose. His consistent, personalised approach led to stronger, more mutually beneficial relationships.

As Adam's reputation as a valuable resource grew, so did his business. He received more referrals and invitations to collaborate on exciting projects. More importantly, he found greater fulfillment in his work. Focusing on giving value and building real connections enabled Adam to feel more aligned with his purpose as a capacity-building consultant, working with clients who understood the value he provided and appreciated his contribution to their own mission.

***

Lessons Learned

Here are the key takeaways from Adam's path to personal growth:

- **Consistency Is Key**

  Sporadic outreach is easily forgotten. Consistent, regular communication keeps you top of mind and demonstrates your reliability.

- **Personalisation Matters**

  Generic mass outreach lacks impact. Tailoring your communication to each person's interests and needs shows that you value the relationship.

- **Give More Than You Take**

  Focus on providing value to your network, not just when you need something but as a continuous habit. Share resources, make introductions and offer support.

- **Be Vulnerable**

  Share your own journey, including the challenges you've faced and what you've learned. This helps you connect on a more human level and builds trust and rapport.

- **Align With Your Purpose**

  Focusing on giving value and building genuine relationships not only strengthens your business but also brings greater fulfillment in your work.

Adam's story shows us that nurturing relationships isn't about convenience but about consistent, personal attention. Giving value, showing vulnerability and staying true to purpose builds strong, mutually beneficial relationships that underpin a thriving consulting business.

***

ACTION STEPS

Nurturing your client relationships is key to long-term success. Here are some action steps to help you strengthen your client bonds:

- Commit time and schedule regular client check-ins.
- Gather and implement client feedback.
- Utilise a personalised approach for each client relationship.
- Establish a method for tracking and celebrating client successes.
- Design a loyalty program or exclusive offerings for long-term clients.
- Set up automated reminders for important client dates and milestones.
- Develop a self-care routine to maintain your own wellbeing.
- Create a process for handling difficult situations or conflicts.
- Establish clear boundaries to maintain work-life balance.

Ready to go deeper? Download the free bonus collection at: www.packagepromotescale.com/bonus

Phase 3: Scale

The final phase of the Package Promote Scale Framework focuses on scaling your consulting business to boost profitability in a way that fits your lifestyle goals. Scaling goes beyond simply bringing in more revenue; it also means crafting a business model that sustains the life you want to live. In this section, you'll learn how to put systems and processes in place to handle growing demand without sacrificing quality or risking burnout. This approach provides you with the ability to grow your business sustainably while maintaining the flexibility to adapt and innovate. Ultimately, this ensures a balanced life as a successful business owner.

Step 7 – Integrate

Integration in business is like piecing together a puzzle. Each piece represents a part of your business – your values, operations and tools – and when they all fit together, the bigger picture comes into focus. It's about creating a seamless experience for everyone who interacts with your business, including yourself. Why integrate? Integration is vital for finding the sweet spot of efficiency and consistency. It's like having a single command centre where every piece of data and every process aligns perfectly with your business vision.

Imagine running a business where every action, every decision, is streamlined. You have tools that handle the repetitive tasks, leaving you free to focus on what you do best. However, it is not only about the tools; it's about how they come together to support your workflow and business goals. This is what's at the heart of integration – everything working in concert, reducing friction and multiplying your effectiveness.

Effective integration starts with a clear outline of your business processes. This is an honest look at what you do and how you do it. From there, you can identify the tools that help you automate, simplify and streamline these processes. However, be aware that there are some pitfalls along the way. Without a clear strategy, you might find yourself pulled in too many directions, wasting resources. And then there's the 'shiny object syndrome' – being tempted by every new tool or opportunity that comes your way, even when they don't serve your bigger picture. simplify and streamline these processes. However, be aware that there are some pitfalls along the way. Without a clear strategy, you might find yourself pulled in too many directions, wasting resources. And then there's the 'shiny object syndrome' – being tempted by every new tool or opportunity that comes your way, even when they don't serve your bigger picture.

Staying focused on your core offerings is vital. When you're tempted to take on work outside your norm because cash flow is tight, for example, pause and consider. Each job needs to meet specific criteria: it must be profitable, enjoyable, within your skillset and something you'd want to repeat. The goal here is empowerment. This means choosing the work that aligns with your business vision and values, not working out of desperation.

Speaking of alignment, every aspect of your business must reflect your core values. From the people you hire to the clients you serve, there must be a harmony that resonates with what you stand for. Sometimes, you'll face resistance – to change, to new tools or to streamlined processes. Yet overcoming these challenges is part of creating a business that's truly integrated.

A business system isn't just a set of tools; it's the synergy between you, your workflow and the technology you adopt. Take Bill, for example. (We'll talk more about Bill in this step's Case Study but, for now, here's a bit of insight to help with the concept of integration.) Bill is a consultant engineer who built his business systems around his expertise and client needs. He chose tools that automated his scheduling and invoicing so he could focus more on his engineering designs. He documented processes so that every project followed a clear path, reducing errors and increasing client satisfaction. For Bill, integration meant setting up a business that worked efficiently, delivered consistently and adapted as it grew.

To establish such a system, you start by pinpointing the needs, evaluating solutions and then meticulously implementing the chosen system. And it's not set in stone; it requires regular assessments and tweaks to ensure it continues to serve your business. Other common pitfalls? These include jumping in without due diligence or getting swayed by complex features you'll never use.

The foundation for success within the Scale phase of the Package Promote Scale Framework, is a well-integrated business. Your tools, your processes and your people – they all need to work together towards a common goal. That's what sets the stage for growth, enabling you to reach and exceed your business aspirations.

***

BEGINNING WITH THE END IN MIND

When you start your business, you have an end goal in mind – a picture of success. It might be a thriving consultancy with a list of satisfied clients, a steady cash flow and a reputation that precedes you. To get there, you need to chart a clear course. That's where integrating your business comes in. It's about lining up your daily operations with that end goal, ensuring each step takes you closer to that vision of success.

Think about the roles in your business. You might start as a one-person show, handling everything from marketing to service delivery. Eventually, you'll need systems allowing your business to operate smoothly even when you step back. This involves more than just technology. It requires setting up processes that anyone can follow. Essentially, you're creating a playbook for your business.

A common trap in business is overservicing clients. You want to give the best but, without clear boundaries, you could be giving away too much of your time without fair return. Your systems help prevent this. They define the scope and make sure both you and the client stick to it, which is crucial for your business to remain profitable and scalable.

Here's how to put the right systems in place:

- **Consider What Your Ideal Work Week Would Look Like**

  Set aside time to focus on specific aspects of your business beyond client work.

- **Identify What You Do Daily, Weekly And Monthly**

  Break down these tasks and decide what's essential and who is responsible. For example, maybe you could outsource tasks such as bookkeeping.

- **Look For The Slow Spots And Trouble Areas In Your Processes**

  What's holding you up? What could be done quicker or more efficiently?

- **Document Every Process**

  This isn't just busywork; it's about understanding how your business operates and finding ways to do it better.

- **Create A Standard Operating Procedure (SOP) For Each Task**

  These can be simple: checklists, quick reference guides or video tutorials, templated emails and proposals. They make your life easier and ensure quality and consistency.

- **Choose Tools That Fit Your SOPs**

  Not every shiny new software will be right for your business. Pick tools that solve a problem and are easy for you and potential team members to use.

Every system and tool you implement needs to resonate with your business values. They must help you deliver the service you're passionate about more effectively.

You may face resistance to change, and that's natural. You'll need to work through your own hesitations and the technical snags you might encounter along the way. Keep your eyes on that picture of success. Don't let new tools or unexpected opportunities distract you unless they align with your long-term goals.

As you build your business systems, keep checking back with your end goal. Are you moving closer to it? Are the systems and tools making your workday smoother? Are they freeing you up to focus more on growth activities? Are they enabling things to move faster? These are the measures of successful integration.

So, as we explore the Scale phase of our framework, keep in mind that a well-integrated business is your platform for growth. It's about working smarter, with a clear vision and the right tools to make it happen. This is how you build a business that becomes a lasting legacy.

***

KNOWING YOUR BUSINESS WORKFLOW

To run your consulting business efficiently, it's essential to know your workflow. A well-documented workflow demonstrates you understand every step involved in your operations from start to finish. It's the backbone of your day-to-day business and helps to ensure nothing falls through the cracks.

Breaking it down, a workflow is the steps you and your team follow to complete tasks and projects. It encompasses the who, what, when, and how of getting things done in your business. The clearer and more streamlined your workflow, the more productive your business can be.

Here's how you can get a handle on your workflow:

- Review your notes from the Test and Refine steps in Phase 1. What did you identify that could be streamlined, improved or eliminated without compromising on quality and results?

- Start by listing all the tasks that need to happen for a typical project or day at your business. This might include responding to client emails, drafting proposals, executing the service you provide or following up invoices.
- Next, organise the tasks on the list in the order they need to happen. This will give you a visual representation or map of your current workflow.
- With this map in hand, you can identify any steps that are taking longer than expected. Maybe you're spending too much time on one task or perhaps there's a particular task that always seems to delay the whole project.
- Ask yourself if there are ways to do these tasks more efficiently. Can any steps be combined? Is there a better time to do certain tasks? Are there any steps you can eliminate?
- Look into automation for repetitive tasks. If you find yourself doing the same thing over and over, there's likely a tool or some software that can automate it for you.
- Think about how each task contributes to your end goals. If a task doesn't help you meet your business objectives, it might be time to re-evaluate why you're doing it.
- Consider if the task needs to be done, are you the best person to do it? What's the financial and opportunity cost of you doing it verses outsourcing or delegating it?
- Be open to changing your processes. Sometimes we resist change because we're comfortable with the way things are. By being flexible and willing to adapt, you can find new, more efficient ways of working.
- If you work with a team, make sure they're all on the same page with the workflow. Clarity and communication are key to ensuring that everyone understands their responsibilities and the order in which tasks need to be completed.
- Finally, once you think you have a good workflow in place, don't forget to test it out. Run through the workflow several times and tweak it as necessary. The goal is to make sure it's

the best it can be for your business needs.

Understanding and refining your workflow is a critical step towards running a more streamlined and successful business. It's about making sure that every task, no matter how small, is carried out efficiently and contributes to the larger goals of your consultancy. Knowing your workflow inside and out allows you to save time, reduce stress, and provide better service to your clients.

***

CREATING STANDARD OPERATING PROCEDURES

It might sound super formal and maybe even a bit boring, but a standard operating procedure (SOP) is actually pretty awesome when it comes to running your business smoothly. Think of SOPs as your business's instruction manual. They're the 'how-tos' for just about everything you do from the moment you start your workday to when you wrap things up.

So why are SOPs so important? Well, they make sure that everyone knows exactly what to do and how to do it. This means that you can deliver the same great service to your clients, every single time. And if you work with a team, SOPs help everyone to stay on the same page. Using SOPs helps you to grow and scale your business, improve the quality of the services you provide and save time!

You might be thinking, *I know what I'm doing, I don't need to write it all down.* But here's the thing: even if you're flying solo, having SOPs can be a game changer. They save you time because you don't have to think about what comes next – you've already laid it all out. And if the day comes when you bring someone else on board, you'll have a ready-made guide to help them hit the ground running.

While there are business consultants who can create SOPs for you using video and screen recording services and transcriptions (we cover this more in detail in Getting Help

When You Need It later in this step), our mantra is done is better than perfect! If you don't have the budget to outsource, just start with what you can do.

How To Put Together Some Great SOPs

Start with your core SOPs. These are the areas that most consultants need documented:

- **Team** (include suppliers, subcontractors, employees).
- **Marketing** (include branding, tone and voice, case studies, events, speaking, writing).
- **Sales** (include sales process, calls, pricing, proposals).
- **Client onboarding and offboarding** (include feedback, reviews, referrals, complaints).
- **Project management and service delivery** (include file management, version control).
- **Technology** (include cyber security, tool selection and tech stack, use of Artificial Intelligence, back up and disaster recovery).
- **Finance and legal compliance** (include due diligence of new clients, use of contracts and agreements, pricing, discounts, pro bono, IP).

Then follow these steps to document each SOP:

- **Begin By Writing Down The Tasks You Do Regularly**

  These could be daily tasks like checking emails, weekly routines like updating your project list or important workflows like onboarding a new client.

- **Take Each Task And Break It Down Into Clear, Simple Steps**

  Write as if someone new is reading it for the first time.

- **Decide The Best Format For Sharing Your SOPs**

  Some may suit a written checklist, others might work better as a short video or annotated screenshots.

- **Review And Update Your SOPs Regularly**

  As your business evolves, your systems will too. Aim to review them monthly or quarterly to keep them relevant.

Here are some other things to consider when creating your SOPs:

- Make sure your SOPs are easy to find. You don't want to have to search through a mountain of files every time you need to look something up.
- Keep them short and sweet. The longer they are, the less likely you and your team are to use them.
- If you're not sure how to start, just pick one task and write a SOP for it. Once you've done one, the others will be easier.
- Using SOPs means you can be confident that nothing gets missed. They're like the checklist pilots use before take-off. It's not that they don't know how to fly the plane, but using the checklist makes sure they don't forget anything important.
- And just like pilots have co-pilots to help them out, you might find that having an accountability buddy can help you stick to your SOPs. This is someone who checks in with you to make sure you're following your procedures and can help you stay on track.
- Create a schedule each month to review a SOP and add new ones.
- If you have a team, get them involved to create SOPs for their areas of responsibility.

By now, you're probably starting to see how valuable SOPs can be. They're not just documents that sit on a shelf collecting dust. They're living, breathing guides that help you run your business better. SOPs take the guesswork out of your day-to-day tasks and free up your mind to focus on the bigger picture – like how to grow your business and take care of your clients.

So, take a little time to start putting together your own SOPs. It might feel like extra work at first, but once you've got them, you'll wonder how you ever managed without them. Plus, you'll be building a strong foundation for your business that will support you as you grow, and that's something to be excited about.

***

SELECTING & IMPLEMENT TOOLS

Selecting and implementing tools for your business is a crucial step. The right tools can help you manage your tasks efficiently, keep track of important information, and communicate effectively with clients and your team. When it comes down to it, these tools are the nuts and bolts that keep the machinery of your business running smoothly.

So, how do you go about choosing the right tools? Think about what tasks take up most of your day. Is there a way to automate these or make them simpler? For example, do you need a better way to schedule meetings or a system that handles invoicing and payments? Whatever it is, make a list of the tasks you think could be done more efficiently.

Here's what to keep in mind when you're tool shopping:

- **Ease of Use**

  You want something that's straightforward. If a tool is too complex, you'll spend more time figuring it out than the time it's supposed to save you.

- **Reliability**

  Look for tools that have good reviews and are known for minimal downtime.

- **Cost-Effectiveness**

  The tool needs to be a good investment for your business, offering more value than the cost required to use it.

Once you've found some potential tools, here's how to get started with them:

- **Test Them Thoroughly**

  Many tools offer a trial period, so use that time to see if the tool fits well with your workflow.

- **Learn How To Use Them Properly**

  Whether through online tutorials, help articles or customer support, ensure you understand all the functionalities the tool offers.

- **Introduce Them To Your Team Gradually**

  If the tool changes how your team works, give everyone time to adjust and learn.

Some common tools you might like to consider include:

- **Communication platforms** – essential for keeping in touch with everyone involved in your business.
- **Accounting software** – to track your finances, from expenses to income.
- **CRM systems** – for managing customer relationships and keeping track of interactions.
- **All-in-one marketing platforms** – for your marketing and promotion needs.
- **Project management software** – to keep your projects organised and on track.
- **Scheduling tools** – for organising your time and making sure you're where you need to be.

Recognise that these tools are there to serve you, not the other way around. They need to take the heavy lifting out of repetitive tasks and free you up to focus on growing your business and delivering quality service to your clients.

Once you've chosen and started using a tool, it's not set in stone. As your business evolves, you might find some tools no longer serve their purpose or that better options have come onto the market. Regularly review the tools you use to ensure they still fit with your business needs.

Carefully selecting and implementing the right tools streamlines your operations, reduces unnecessary manual work, and gives you the space to focus on the strategic side of your business. It's all about finding what works for you and using it to its fullest potential.

***

LEVERAGING YOUR BUSINESS SYSTEMS

Leveraging your business systems means making the most of the tools and processes you've put in place. It's about using them to work more efficiently. When you've got good systems, they help you figure out which tasks are most important, which can be done quicker and which you might not need to do at all.

To leverage your business systems effectively, you'll want to keep a few things in mind:

- Understand what your systems are capable of. If you've got a project management tool, get to know all its features. You might find it can do things you hadn't thought of that can save you time.
- Keep an eye on the data your systems are collecting. This could be sales numbers, website visitors, customer feedback – all sorts of useful information. This data can help you make smart decisions about where to take your business next.
- Use your systems to manage your time better. This means setting clear deadlines for yourself and sticking to them. And if you have a team, it means making sure everyone knows who's doing what and by when.

Here's how to make sure you're leveraging your systems the right way:

- **Set Clear Goals**

  What do you want your business to achieve? Do you want

more sales? Would you like to improve customer service? No matter what your goals are, your systems need to help you get there.

- **Prioritise Your Tasks**

  Not all tasks are created equal. Some things are going to move you towards your goals faster than others. Focus on those first.

- **Don't Get Distracted**

  It's easy to get sidetracked by new tools or tasks that seem urgent but aren't really that important. Stick to your plan and your systems. Keep a Post-it® note on your computer screen with the three priorities for your business and the things you won't do, such as signing up for webinars just out of interest!

- **Keep Your SOPs Up To Date**

  If you've found a better way to do something, update your SOPs to reflect that. And if a system isn't working for you anymore, it might be time to find a new one.

- **Have An Accountability System**

  This could be a weekly check in with yourself or with a team member to make sure you're following your systems and making progress towards your goals.

When you're using your business systems well, they help you stay focused on the things that matter. They take away the guesswork and let you be more creative because you're not always worried about what you might be forgetting. They help you provide a consistent service to your clients because you're doing things the same effective way every time. And they help you grow your business because you're always looking for ways to do things better.

Setting up your business systems to their full potential can take your business to the next level. With good systems on your side, you'll be amazed at what you can achieve.

GETTING HELP WHEN YOU NEED IT

When you're running a business, there's no shame in admitting that sometimes you need a helping hand. It's a sign of strength, not weakness, to recognise when you're out of your depth and could use some expertise. After all, you can't be an expert in everything!

Getting help when you need it is smart business. Think about it. You hire a plumber to fix a leaky pipe because they know what they're doing. It's the same with your business. Sometimes you might need an IT expert to set up your network and other times it could be a business process improvement consultant to help you streamline your operations. Either way, buying in expertise will still require you to have input, some workshops and 'brain dumping'. You need to account for the time and cost involved in this. Getting a task done and off your to-do list can be a motivating factor in engaging a professional, just like your clients engage you for your expertise as a consultant.

Here's how you can go about getting the right kind of help:

- **Identify What You Need Help With**

  Is the task tech related? Is it about growing your business? Make a list of areas where you think an expert could make a big difference.

- **Look For The Right Person**

  You want someone who is both skilled and a good fit for your business. They need to understand what you are about and be someone you can envision working with.

- **Check Their Credentials And Experience**

  You want to make sure they really know their stuff and have a good track record to prove it.

- **Ask Around**

  Get recommendations from people you trust. If someone you

know has had a positive interaction with a specialist, that's a good sign.

- **Talk To Them**

   Before you hire anyone, have a chat with them. Ask them about their approach, how they work and what they think they can do for your business.

- **Start Small**

   Maybe give them a minor project to start with, just to see how it goes. If they do a good job, you can think about bringing them on for bigger things.

Here's why getting help is so important:

- **It Frees Up Your Time**

   When someone else is taking care of the tech stuff or the admin tasks, that's more time you have to focus on the big picture stuff.

- **It Brings New Ideas**

   Specialists come with their own set of knowledge and insights. They can suggest things you might not have thought of.

- **It Helps You Grow**

   With the right help, you can take your business to new heights. You can take on more work, offer new services and improve the services you already offer.

- **It Takes The Pressure Off**

   Running a business is hard work. Knowing you have experts you can rely on can take a load off your mind.

The goal is to make your business the best it can be. Sometimes, that means bringing in people with the skills and know-how to help you get there. So, don't hesitate to reach out for help when you need it. It's a smart move that can pay off big time for your business.

CONCLUSION

As we wrap up this step on integrating your business systems, let's take a moment to reflect on what we've covered. From understanding your workflow to creating SOPs, selecting the right tools and knowing when to reach out for help, each step is about setting up your business for success.

Integration isn't just about getting your ducks in a row; it's about making sure those ducks are working for you, helping you move faster and smarter. When you integrate well, every part of your business communicates with the other parts. It's like a team where everyone knows their role and how to play it well.

You might be thinking, *That's a lot to take in*. And you're right, it is. But you don't have to do it all at once. Take it step by step:

- Start by looking at your daily tasks and figure out where you can save time.
- Write down your processes and think about how you can make them clearer and more efficient.
- Pick out tools that fit your needs and budget and take the time to learn them inside out.
- And when you feel stuck or overwhelmed, don't be afraid to ask for help.

By now, you will ideally have a solid understanding of why good business systems are essential. They help you stay organised, save time and give you the freedom to focus on what really matters—growing your business and taking care of your clients.

When you are putting you've learned into practice, keep in mind the bigger picture. Every system you implement, every tool you use, and every bit of help you receive needs to bring you closer to your ultimate goal. It could be expanding your client base, launching a new service or maybe even taking a bit more time off to spend with family and friends.

As you move forward, think about how you can apply what you've learned here to your business. How can you make your systems work better for you? How can you use your tools more effectively? Who can you reach out to for help?

Running a business is an ongoing commitment filled with challenges. There will be ups and downs, but with the right systems in place, you'll be well-equipped to navigate whatever comes your way. Each step you take strengthens your business, making it more resilient for the future.

***

CASE STUDY

Bill, a consultant engineer, was at a crossroads. His business was growing but so was the chaos. He found himself overwhelmed with all the project documents, endless email chains and the constant struggle to keep his projects on track. Bill knew that to take his consultancy to the next level, he needed to integrate his business systems.

One of the main challenges Bill faced was the lack of a centralised project management system. Client requirements, design files and progress updates were scattered across various email threads and local folders. This disorganisation led to missed deadlines, confusion among project team members and a general sense of inefficiency. All of this left Bill feeling despondent about his circumstances. He wondered whether a recent offer of a high-paying, full-time job was a good way out.

Another issue was Bill's manual invoicing and bookkeeping processes. He spent countless hours each month generating invoices and reconciling expenses, detracting from his core engineering work.

Determined to overcome these hurdles, Bill sought tools and processes to streamline operations. He researched project management software, seeking a solution that could handle his engineering projects' complexity while being user-friendly.

After careful consideration, Bill implemented a cloud-based project management system. He decided to pay a specialist provider to migrate all his current projects into the new system, creating clear timelines, task assignments and communication channels. Bill also trained his team how to use the software effectively.

To address his invoicing and bookkeeping challenges, Bill invested in an integrated accounting software that could automatically generate invoices from tracked project hours and expenses. He also outsourced his bookkeeping, quarterly Business Activity Statement (BAS) generation and BAS submission to the tax office. Bill synced this software with his project management system, ensuring that all billable time and costs were accurately captured.

Bill also took the time to document his key processes, creating SOPs and simple checklists for everything from client onboarding to project closeout. He made these SOPs and checklists easily accessible to his team through a shared knowledge base. He also taught his team how to create SOPs.

The impact of these changes was swift and notable. With a centralised project management system, Bill and his team had a clear, real-time view of every project's status. Communication improved, deadlines were met more consistently and client satisfaction increased.

The automated invoicing and bookkeeping saved Bill numerous hours each month, giving him more time to focus on the high-value consultation work he was known for and which he loved the most. It also provided a clearer picture of his business's financial health, enabling better decision-making.

Most importantly, the new systems and processes gave Bill a sense of control and confidence in his business. He no longer felt like he was constantly putting out fires, but rather, he was proactively steering his consultancy towards success.

Lessons Learned

Here are the key takeaways from Bill's path to personal growth:

- **Centralisation Is Crucial**

  A centralised system that houses all key information and communication can dramatically improve efficiency and reduce confusion.

- **Automation Saves Time**

  Automating repetitive tasks like invoicing and bookkeeping can save significant time and provide a clearer financial picture, allowing you to respond to potential issues in a timely manner.

- **Document Processes**

  Creating SOPs and checklists that are easily accessible provides a consistent and aligned approach and reduces the challenges associated with working in an ad hoc way.

- **Choose User-Friendly Tools**

  When selecting software, don't just look at the features or the price but also consider the user-friendliness for you, your team and clients.

- **Integration Enables Control**

  Integrating systems and processes gives you a greater sense of control and confidence within your business.

Bill's story demonstrates that by taking the time to integrate key systems and processes, you will not only improve efficiency and client satisfaction but will also achieve greater control in your business.

***

ACTION STEPS

Integrating your business systems is crucial for streamlining your operations and improving efficiency. Follow these action steps to create a seamless workflow:

- Map out your main business workflows.
- Identify areas of inefficiency or redundancy in your processes.
- Create SOPs for key business tasks.
- Research and select tools to streamline your operations.
- Implement a centralised project management system.
- Develop a systematic approach for client onboarding and offboarding.
- Create templates for common documents and communications.
- Set up a system for tracking and analysing key performance metrics.

Ready to go deeper? Download the free bonus collection at: www.packagepromotescale.com/bonus

Step 8 – Amplify

Imagine your consulting business is flourishing. Your clients are happy, your calendar is full and you're making the impact and profits you've always aimed for. But with success comes a new challenge: your workload has outgrown the hours in your day. The solution? It's time to amplify.

Amplifying is about boosting your business's capabilities and capacity. It means taking the solid foundation you've built and expanding it, allowing you to serve more clients and increase your impact. And to do that, you'll likely need to grow your team.

Let's explore what we mean by 'your team'. This is the group of people you collaborate with to deliver outstanding results. It includes the internal team members you might hire and the external partnerships you might form. Each person, whether in-house or external, plays a pivotal role in your business's ability to prosper and expand.

Understanding the difference between internal and external teams is essential. Internal teams are those dedicated individuals you bring on board as part-time or full-time staff. External teams, on the other hand, consist of collaborators or subcontractors you partner with to complement your services.

It's crucial to acknowledge a common trap here: burnout. It's dangerously easy to fall into the mindset that you can handle everything on your own. This solo approach can have serious consequences for you, your business, your clients, and everyone connected to them. Recognise your limits and know when it's time to ask for help. Finding the right people takes time, so it's wise to start before you hit a crunch point. Waiting until the last minute often means making hasty, and not always the best, decisions. Don't be the single point of failure in your business where the sales pipeline and service delivery all rely on you.

Many consultants resist delegating or collaborating due to a desire to maintain control or a belief that perfection can only be achieved if they handle everything themselves. However, this can be counterproductive. Leadership requires knowing when to delegate, when to find others who complement your expertise and when to take the helm. Reflect on your strengths: Are you the visionary leader or the star player who shines brightest in client interactions? What possibilities could open up by doing things differently? Maybe it's time to consider bringing on an operations manager, online business manager or similar support.

Transitioning from solo work to a team-based approach comes with its own set of challenges. Here are some strategies to ease the shift:

- Start with trust and build from there.
- Create a culture of mutual respect and support.
- Keep communication open, frequent and clear.
- Align on shared values and goals for a cohesive direction.

There are several methods to amplify your business's capabilities:

- Leverage your professional networks to find talent and opportunities.
- Form strategic collaborations that complement your

strengths.
- Engage with subcontractors to handle specialised tasks.
- Consider outsourcing to manage costs effectively and efficiently.
- Hire staff when you're ready to build an internal team.

When considering these options, ask yourself: Which method is most appropriate for your business? It's a decision that comes from a deep understanding of your business's current state, your personal goals and market conditions.

In this step, we'll consider the nuances of expanding your team – from collaborating with peers to outsourcing and hiring. We'll cover how to make these critical decisions and how to implement them in a way that aligns with your business's core values and mission.

***

EXPLORING DIFFERENT WAYS TO AMPLIFY

Growing your consulting business means more than adding more clients or working longer hours. It means smart growth—enhancing your ability to serve without stretching yourself too thin. There are different ways to amplify your operations, and choosing the right path can make all the difference.

Collaborate

First, let's discuss collaborating. You're great at what you do but you recognise that collaborating with other consultants could bring a fresh perspective and additional expertise to your projects. Rather than losing your identity in the mix, it's about complementing your strengths with the strengths of others. Partnering up allows you to take on larger projects, enter new markets, and offer a more comprehensive service package suite to your clients. Collaboration is a give and take that, when done right, can lead to mutual growth and success.

Outsource

Next up is outsourcing. This is about finding individuals or organisations that can take on certain tasks for you. It could be anything from administrative duties to specialised services that fall outside your expertise. Outsourcing allows you to focus on what you do best while ensuring that all the other work is handled efficiently and professionally. It's a way to tap into a pool of specialised skills and potential cost savings. Think of it as delegation on a broader scale, where you remain in the driver's seat but have a team of specialists contributing to your progress.

Hire

Then there's the option of hiring. This could mean bringing on part-time or full-time staff. Hiring is about building your internal team, people who will grow with your business and contribute to its culture and success over the long term. It's a significant commitment that involves finding the right people who share your vision and values and setting them up for success. You'll need to think about things such as employment laws, contracts and workspace, but the pay-off is having a dedicated team aligned with your mission.

As you consider these options, reflect on a few key points:

- Which areas of your business could benefit the most from additional support?
- Do you need help temporarily for a specific project or are you looking for a more permanent solution?
- Are there tasks that you're not an expert in or simply don't enjoy that could be outsourced?
- What's the financial picture? Hiring staff is a different kind of investment than, say, outsourcing.

These aren't decisions to rush into. It's like piecing together a puzzle; each piece must fit just right. And it's okay to start small. Maybe you could begin by outsourcing a few tasks to free up some of your time, or perhaps you can try collaborating on a project before considering a more formal partnership.

Given the potential pitfalls in employment regulations, we urge you to consult a legal expert on what's relevant and important to you in your business. For example, in Australia there are specific industrial relations laws and obligations for independent contractors and employees.

The Fair Work Ombudsman website has helpful information, and we recommend that you also seek advice from your accountant, human resources consultants, business advisers and small business lawyers.

If you choose to **collaborate or outsource**, here are some simple steps to guide you:

- **Define The Role You Need Filled**

  What skills and qualities are essential for the job?

- **Look For Recommendations**

  Your network can be a great resource for finding trustworthy collaborators and subcontractors.

- **Vet Applicants Carefully**

  It is crucial to consider their track record, reliability and ability to deliver on time and to standard.

- **Set Clear Terms**

  Make sure expectations, deadlines and deliverables are understood by everyone involved.

- **Consider Profit Margins**

  Examine your pricing and profit margins, perform cashflow forecasts and ensure that you have factored in additional time and costs while still making a profit and paying yourself.

For those looking to **hire**, consider these steps:

- **Identify The Gap In Your Team**

  What role would have the most significant impact on your business?

- **Create A Clear Job Description**

  Know what you're looking for and communicate it effectively.

- **Screen Candidates Thoroughly**

  Look for skills, expertise, cultural fit, and shared values.

- **Onboard With Care**

  Help new hires understand their role, your business and the larger mission they're now a part of.

Regardless of the path you choose, communication is your best friend. Be clear about what you want to achieve and be open to receiving feedback. This is how you build a team – be it internal, external or a mix – that's robust, flexible and aligned with your goals.

Think about the bigger picture. Amplifying your business enhances your ability to make a meaningful impact rather than simply growing for the sake of growth. It's about creating a work environment that allows for creativity, innovation and personal development. And at the heart of it, it's about ensuring that your business continues to serve your clients in the best way possible while also maintaining the quality of life you seek.

So, take a moment to consider this: How could your business benefit from a little amplification? Whether it's through collaboration, outsourcing or hiring, there are many routes to explore. The right choice is the one that aligns with your personal and business goals, creating a harmonious balance that supports sustainable growth.

***

IDENTIFYING AND BUILDING COLLABORATIONS

Building collaborations and finding the right partners to walk alongside you is like opening your business to new horizons. When you decide to collaborate, you're not just sharing tasks; you're sharing a vision. This section will guide you through identifying and forming these critical partnerships.

First, clarity is key. Know what you want from a collaboration. Is it to expand your service offerings, enter new markets or simply manage your workload better? Start with a clear picture of the role your collaborators will play. Don't restrict this to looking for a one-size-fits-all partner. Instead, look to find someone who complements your strengths and fills in the gaps where needed.

Here's how to approach it:

- **List The Skills And Qualities That You Consider Essential In Your Collaborators**

  They need to bring something to the table that you don't possess, whether it's a skill set, market presence or a fresh perspective.

- **Have An Ideal Collaborator Profile In Mind**

  It's about their capabilities and how well you connect with them. After all, collaboration is as much about the relationship as it is about business.

- **Utilise Your Network**

  Your existing contacts are invaluable. They know you, and they might know just the person or company you need. A simple post on LinkedIn or an email to your contacts can open doors you didn't even know existed.

- **Ask For Help**

  Some consultancy groups or agencies have a range of pre-vetted consultants who they work with and who may be able to help you on a short-term or long-term basis.

When you've found some potential collaborators, vetting them is crucial. You're entrusting them with your business's reputation and your clients' trust. Here are some factors to keep in mind:

- **Assess Their Trustworthiness And Reliability**

  Can they deliver what they promise, and do they do so consistently?

- **Evaluate Their Quality Of Work**

  Their standards need to meet or exceed your own.

- **Review Client Satisfaction**

  What do their past clients say about their work?

- **Look For A Proactive Collaboration**

  Are they proactive and reliable or do they expect you to manage them, delegate and follow-up?

- **Consider Compatibility**

  Your work styles need to complement each other.

- **Confirm The Essentials**

  Ensure they have the capacity to take on the work you're considering and that they – and you – are adequately insured.

- **Seek Out Collaborators With Shared Values**

  This can make or break a collaboration. You need to be on the same page when it comes to the things that matter most.

Once you've found someone who ticks all these boxes, it's time to talk structure. How will the collaboration work on a practical level?

- **Draft A Collaboration Agreement**

  It's essential to outline the terms of your partnership. What are the expectations, responsibilities, project management, client facing roles and boundaries? Getting these down on paper isn't just about legalities; it's about ensuring everyone is clear and agrees on the partnership's framework.

- **Maintain Independence**

  While you're working closely together, preserving your autonomy is important. You both have brands and reputations to uphold.

- **Discuss How You'll Handle IP And Confidentiality**

  Protecting your business interests is not about mistrust; it's about professionalism and foresight.

- **Seek Legal Advice**

  We recommend that you consult a lawyer for your collaboration agreement. As tempting as it might be to cut and paste agreements from elsewhere, it's likely that it will be inadequate for your needs. Some small business legal firms also have template agreements you can purchase and offer customisation services, where they customise existing agreements, making it less expensive than starting from scratch. Allow plenty of time to find the right provider. Some have waitlists or charge extra for urgent work.

And what about when things don't go as planned? Having a strategy for managing disagreements, disputes or unexpected challenges is part of a robust collaboration. Address issues early, communicate openly and always aim for a resolution that strengthens the relationship.

The beauty of collaboration is in its mutual benefit. When chosen wisely, these partnerships can open avenues for growth that you might never have been able to manage alone. They can be a source of support, innovation and strength. The goal is to create a team that is greater than the sum of its parts and where both you and your collaborators grow and succeed together.

Collaborations are founded upon mutually beneficial relationships, not transactional interactions. They need to be nurtured with the same care and consideration you give to your clients. Regular check-ins, shared celebrations of milestones and a willingness to adapt as you go along will help keep the partnership vibrant and productive.

As we wrap up this section, take a moment to reflect on your current network. Who do you know that could become a valuable collaborator? Start the conversation and begin exploring the potential. Your next successful partnership could be just one discussion away.

***

OUTSOURCING FOR BUSINESS BENEFIT

Outsourcing can be a game changer in the consulting world. It's about recognising that you don't have to be the jack-of-all-trades. Instead, you can bring in people with specialised skills for specific tasks, often providing more flexibility and sometimes at a lower cost than if you tried to do everything in-house.

So, what exactly is outsourcing? Simply put, it's when you hire external resources to handle tasks or projects that are outside your expertise or capacity. Think of it as enlisting a specialist to do what they do best, allowing you to focus on your core services and growing your business.

The benefits of outsourcing are numerous. It can provide:

- Access to specialised skills and expertise.
- Cost savings, particularly if the tasks are outsourced to individuals or firms with efficient processes or lower operating costs.
- The opportunity to tap into remote workers in other locations including offshore.
- High-quality results, especially when the task requires expertise that you or your team don't possess.
- The flexibility to scale services up or down according to project needs or client demands.

- More time for you to focus on strategy, client acquisition and other high-value activities.

So, what can you outsource? The list is quite extensive, but some common examples are:

- Administrative tasks that are necessary but time-consuming, like data entry or transcriptions.
- Specialised tasks that require expertise you don't have, such as legal advice or graphic design.
- Time-sensitive tasks that need more hands to meet a deadline without compromising your ongoing projects.

As you consider outsourcing, here are steps to ensure a smooth process:

- **Identify The Provider**

  Look for someone with the expertise and a track record to match.

- **Check Their History**

  Don't skip on checking references and examples of past work.

- **Be Clear**

  Make sure contracts outline deliverables, deadlines and payment terms.

- **Monitor Performance**

  Keep an eye on progress to make sure that the work meets your standards.

It's essential to choose providers who share your commitment to quality and have values that align with yours. This helps to ensure that the work they do for you will meet the high standards your clients expect.

Trust also plays a crucial role here. You need to have confidence that the people you outsource to will treat your projects with the same care and commitment that you do. This means finding someone with the right skills who also fits into the ethos of your business.

However, outsourcing isn't without its challenges. You may face hurdles like:

- Selecting the right provider from a multitude of options.
- Feeling ready to outsource when you are used to working solo.
- Managing costs to ensure that outsourcing remains a financially sound choice.
- Handling cashflow challenges and potential delays in payments from clients.
- Ensuring that deliverables are met on time and to the standard you expect.
- Communicating effectively with providers to avoid misunderstandings.
- Keeping clients happy, which sometimes means managing their perceptions and expectations when it comes to subcontracted work.

To avoid common pitfalls:

- **Communicate Clearly And Regularly**

  Never assume the provider knows exactly what you want.

- **Have A Solid Agreement In Place**

  Start every engagement with a clear agreement that addresses the scope of work, deadlines, payments and any other expectations.

- **Be Proactive**

  Don't wait for a problem to arise before you check on progress.

- **Stay Involved In The Process**

  Outsourcing doesn't mean washing your hands of the task.

When considering outsourcing options, consider your guiding principles. Does the provider understand and respect your mission? Are they committed to continuous improvement? Do they communicate authentically and effectively? These considerations are as vital as their technical skills.

Embracing outsourcing acknowledges that collaboration and effective delegation are key to sustainable growth. You're taking a purpose-driven step to ensure that every aspect of your business operates at its best, even the parts you entrust to others.

In concluding this section, reflect on your current operations. Where could you benefit from the support of specialised professionals? Begin to explore the possibilities. Outsourcing can be your ally in building a business that not only survives but thrives.

***

HIRING TO GROW YOUR INTERNAL TEAM (WHEN THE TIME IS RIGHT)

Hiring is a big step. It's the transition from solo flyer to captain of a larger ship. When your business reaches the stage where you're consistently looking for extra hands to help keep up with demand, it might be time to consider growing your internal team.

Why hire? Because sometimes, the expertise you require is for ongoing needs rather than a single project. Bringing on part-time or full-time staff is about investing in people who will invest their energy back into your business. It's a mutual commitment to growth, not only in terms of revenue but also in knowledge, service quality and reputation.

When you decide to hire, you're doing more than filling a seat. You're looking for someone to carry a piece of your business vision forward. It goes beyond skill sets and experience and is about finding the right fit. Here's what to consider:

- **Alignment With Your Business Values And Vision**

  You want team members who are onboard with where you're headed and why.

- **A Shared Commitment To Your Business Objectives**

  Every new hire needs to be a piece in the larger puzzle of your mission.

- **The Ability To Grow And Adapt With Your Business**

  As your business evolves, so too must your team.

The hiring process involves multiple steps:

- **Identify Your Needs First**

  What roles are essential, and what skills are required to fulfil them?

- **Write A Meaningful Job Description**

  Create a job description that captures the responsibilities and necessary qualifications as well as the heart and soul of your business culture.

- **Screen Candidates Thoughtfully**

  Look for those who not only have the skills but also the demeanour and drive that match your business ethos.

- **Onboard With Intention**

  This is where the true integration begins. More than just training, this means welcoming someone into the fold and setting them up for success.

Hiring is more than a process; it's a relationship that begins the moment you decide to expand your team. It requires nurturing, attention and a willingness to grow together. Here's how you can foster a positive hiring atmosphere:

- **Be Clear From The Start**

  Be clear and upfront about expectations from the start.

- **Encourage Open Communication**

  It's vital in building trust and identifying any issues early on.

- **Support Their Success**

  Provide the tools and support necessary for your team to succeed. This could be anything from a robust onboarding process to continuous professional development opportunities.

Considerations like employment laws, contracts, benefits and work location are also part of the equation. They may seem daunting, but they're manageable with the right approach and resources. As previously mentioned, it's wise to seek professional advice from human resources consultants, lawyers and accountants. These experts can help you manage the complexities of employment and ensure you're not only compliant but also creating a fair and motivating work environment.

The risks and responsibilities of hiring are real but so are the rewards.

Expanding your internal team allows you to:

- Build a dedicated workforce that's in it for the long term.
- Foster a collaborative environment where ideas can flourish.
- Share the workload, which can improve your service offering and client satisfaction.

As you consider hiring, ask yourself a few questions:

- Are you ready to lead a team, and do you have the right support structures in place to do so effectively?
- Is your business financially prepared for the commitment of regular salaries and potential benefits?
- How will you maintain the balance between providing direction and allowing autonomy?

Hiring goes beyond meeting immediate needs and includes planning for the future. Each person you bring on board contributes to a future where your business embodies the collective achievements of a dedicated team.

As we wrap up this section, reflect on the growth and direction of your business. If you're at a point where hiring seems like the next logical step, approach it with intention and care. Your team is your business's greatest asset. Investing in the right people can be the catalyst for sustained success and a deeper impact on the clients you serve.

***

WORKING TOGETHER EFFECTIVELY

The cornerstone of a thriving business is having a team that works together effectively. Once you have the right people on board, whether they're in-house employees, subcontractors or collaborators, it's important to foster a work environment where everyone can do their best work.

Important factors for working together effectively include:

- **Culture**

  Cultivate a positive work culture rooted in shared values and a united vision. Ensure every team member is aligned with the mission and understands the importance of their role. This fosters a sense of passion and investment in their work.

- **Business Planning**

  Adopt a team-centric approach to business planning. Collaboratively set goals and milestones, leveraging the team's collective insights and knowledge. This creates a sense of shared ownership and drives engagement.

- **Tools**

  Choose tools that enhance team efficiency. Use project management software to stay on track and communication platforms to maintain connectivity, which is particularly vital for remote teams. Provide necessary equipment to demonstrate your commitment to each team member's contribution and wellbeing.

- **Communication**

  Treat communication as the lifeline of team efficiency. Engage in meaningful conversations and use feedback loops to transform discussions into opportunities for growth. Follow-up on feedback to show dedication to improving collectively.

- **Meetings**

  Make meetings count by setting clear agendas and objectives. They need to serve as productive sessions that leave team members with a clear understanding of their next steps and how they contribute to the team's objectives.

Other important considerations include:

- **Conflict**

  Approach conflicts with empathy and a solutions-oriented mindset. Establish an open environment for addressing concerns, which can strengthen team bonds and prevent minor misunderstandings from becoming significant issues.

- **Performance**

  View performance monitoring as a tool for guiding team development. Regular reviews need to celebrate achievements and address any challenges constructively, reinforcing the notion of a united team striving for common goals.

- **Diversity**

  Appreciate each person's background and perspective to foster an environment that enhances problem-solving and innovation.

When the team dynamic isn't quite right, take a step back to evaluate it and make adjustments. Sometimes, realignment with core values and goals is needed; other times, more substantial changes may be necessary. Keep an open mind and stay committed to nurturing a positive, productive team environment.

Effective teamwork is about creating a cohesive unit where every member feels valued and the shared mission and goals are clear. Focusing on open communication, providing the right tools, and addressing challenges proactively builds a team that works well together and gets great results for your clients and business.

***

STRATEGICALLY REINVESTING IN YOUR BUSINESS

Strategically reinvesting in your business is how you honour your commitment to its success and longevity. This approach involves making well-thought-out decisions to channel profits into areas that will strengthen and broaden your business's capabilities. It's a proactive measure to secure the future, ensuring that your business adapts, stays relevant and consistently leads the way in meeting and exceeding client expectations.

Key considerations for strategic reinvestment include:

- **Continual Learning**

  This isn't just about keeping pace with industry changes; it's about nurturing a workplace where growth and learning are integral. Investing in your team's development through ongoing education positions your business to meet future challenges with expertise and assurance.

- **Infrastructure**

  The backbone of your operation, your infrastructure is crucial to the business's growth. Investing in updated technology and software not only improves the efficiency of your operations but also elevates the quality of service you offer, demonstrating your commitment to excellence to your team and clients.

- **Innovation**

  Allocating funds for research and development is essential. It's about empowering your team to innovate and paying attention to your clients' needs. This strategy ensures that your offerings meet current demands and drive the market forward, setting new standards. Keep informed about tax incentives and grants for innovation.

- **Financial Health**

  The foundation of strategic reinvestment lies in the financial wellbeing of your business. Meticulous monitoring of cash flow and a deep understanding of the returns on your investments are vital to ensure that your business remains financially robust as it grows. It's about striking the right balance between what you can reinvest and the necessary investments that propel your business ahead.

- **Values And Mission**

  Your reinvestment efforts need to mirror the heart of your business – the core values and mission that set you apart. Growth is meaningful when it aligns with the original vision for your business and continues to create the impact you envisage.

Strategic reinvestment is a continuous, thoughtful process that needs to be aligned with a deep understanding of your business goals. It's not merely a matter of expenditure; it's a deliberate investment in the future success and enduring prosperity of your business. With a methodical and purpose-driven approach to reinvestment, you're investing in the groundwork for the sustained success of your business.

***

CONCLUSION

As we reach the end of this step, it's clear that amplifying your business isn't just about growing bigger—it's about growing smarter and more sustainably. It's about understanding when and how to extend your capabilities, whether through collaboration, outsourcing or hiring. Each strategy has its benefits, and the best choice depends on your business situation, needs, and goals.

Amplification is a sign that you're ready to move beyond the day-to-day grind and shape a future that's not limited by the number of hours you can work in a week. It's a commitment to scale your operations in a way that aligns with your vision for your business and the values that underpin everything you do. It's not about adding more to your plate; it's about enriching what's already there, ensuring each piece works in harmony with the rest.

When thinking about expanding your team, whether internally or externally, be sure to:

- Foster a culture that's grounded in shared values and a clear vision, creating an environment where everyone (employees, subcontractors and collaborators) feels invested in the business's success.
- Approach business planning as a team activity, setting collaborative goals and strategies that reflect the collective wisdom and insights of the group.
- Select tools and technology that will streamline operations, improve communication and enhance productivity, contributing to a more cohesive and efficient workflow.
- Maintain open lines of communication, where feedback is not only encouraged but acted upon, ensuring that every voice is heard and valued.
- Handle conflicts with empathy and a solution-focused mindset, preserving the integrity of your team and the

quality of your work.

When it comes to amplifying your business, it's also crucial to:

- Monitor performance regularly, providing feedback that recognises good work and constructively addresses areas for improvement.
- Welcome diversity, understanding that a variety of backgrounds, perspectives and skills only strengthens your team's ability to innovate and solve problems.
- Stay flexible and willing to reassess and adjust your approach when things aren't working as expected, always keeping the long-term success of the team and business in mind.

Strategic reinvestment is the final piece of the puzzle. It's about putting your profits to work in a way that not only boosts your immediate capabilities but also sets you up for future success. Whether it's through continual learning, infrastructure upgrades or fostering innovation, each reinvestment decision needs to be made with an eye towards the future.

In wrapping up this step, consider how you can amplify your business. It's about more than just growth; it's about building a resilient, adaptive and client-focused enterprise. With a thoughtful approach to expanding your team and capabilities, you're positioning yourself for long-term success in business.

***

CASE STUDY

James, a training curriculum designer, was passionate about helping organisations transform their expertise into engaging, impactful courses. As his consultancy grew, he recognised the need to expand his team to meet the increasing demand for his services.

One of the specific challenges James faced was maintaining the quality and depth of his course content while scaling his operations. When collaborating with freelancers or outsourcing tasks, he often found that the final product lacked the nuance and relevance required to truly resonate with the intended audience.

Another issue James faced was ensuring that all team members, whether internal or external, were aligned with the mission and values of his consultancy. He believed that a shared commitment to delivering transformative learning opportunities was essential to the success of his projects.

To address these challenges, James implemented a number of approaches to amplify his consultancy's capabilities.

To start with, James focused on building a core internal team that embodied his values and mission. He refined his hiring process to assess not only technical skills but also alignment with his vision. James conducted value-alignment exercises during interviews and prioritised candidates who demonstrated a genuine passion for learning and development.

Next, James established a robust onboarding and training program for his team. He created a comprehensive manifesto that clearly articulated the mission, values and approach of his consultancy. This provided valuable guidance for all team members, ensuring that everyone was working towards the same goals. James also implemented regular training sessions to deepen his team's understanding of the mission and enhance their technical skills.

To maintain the quality of his course content, James developed a rigorous quality control process. He set up a peer review system where team members provided constructive feedback on each other's work, ensuring alignment with the mission and adherence to best practices. James also conducted a final review of every course before release to ensure that it met the standards he had set for his business.

In addition to building his internal team, James did his best to leverage collaborations and partnerships to increase the capacity and capability of his consultancy. He identified subject matter experts who could bring depth and relevance to the course content. Collaborating with these experts allowed James to create courses that truly resonated with the intended audience and delivered meaningful results.

James also explored outsourcing opportunities for tasks that didn't require his team's core expertise. He carefully vetted potential providers, selecting those who demonstrated a commitment to quality and a willingness to align with his consultancy's values. Outsourcing these tasks freed up James's internal team to focus on the high-value, mission-critical work that set his consultancy apart.

The impact of these changes was significant. With a dedicated, mission-aligned team and a network of expert collaborators, James was able to scale his operations while maintaining the depth and quality of his course content. His clients noticed the difference, praising the relevance and impact of the learning programs he delivered.

Internally, James's team thrived under the culture of continuous improvement and open dialogue. They felt a deep sense of ownership and pride in their work, knowing they were making a meaningful difference in the lives of learners. This increased their motivation and drove even better results for the business.

For James, the process of amplifying his consultancy was not only financially rewarding but also personally fulfilling. Staying true to his mission and values while strategically expanding his capabilities allowed him to build a thriving business that made a real impact in the field of learning and development.

***

Lessons Learned

Here are the key takeaways from James's path to personal growth:

- **Build A Mission-Aligned Team**

  Surround yourself with team members who share your values and are committed to your mission. This alignment is essential for maintaining quality and consistency as you grow.

- **Invest In Onboarding And Training**

  Develop a comprehensive onboarding program that immerses new team members in your mission and values. Provide ongoing training to deepen their understanding and enhance their skills.

- **Implement Rigorous Quality Control**

  Establish a robust quality control process that includes peer review and final oversight. This ensures that every deliverable meets your high standards and aligns with your mission.

- **Leverage Collaborations And Partnership**

  Identify people and organisations who can bring greater depth and relevance to your offerings. Collaborate with them to expand your capabilities and deliver greater value to your clients.

- **Outsource Strategically**

  Carefully select tasks that can be outsourced to trusted partners who align with your values. This frees up your internal team to focus on the high-value work that sets your consultancy apart.

- **Cultivate A Culture Of Continuous Improvement**

  Foster a culture of open dialogue, constructive feedback and continuous learning. Encourage your team to take ownership of their work and strive for excellence in all they do.

In applying these lessons, you can amplify your impact, scale your operations and build a thriving business that makes a meaningful difference in the lives of those you serve.

***

ACTION STEPS

Amplifying your business's capabilities requires a strategic approach to growth, focusing on expanding your team, enhancing your skills and scaling your operations. Follow these action steps to expand your capacity and reach:

- Conduct a skills gap analysis for your business.
- Develop criteria for identifying potential collaborators or team members.
- Establish a system for vetting and onboarding new team members.
- Develop a communication protocol for remote or distributed teams.
- Get comfortable with delegating tasks and responsibilities.
- Track team performance and productivity.
- Develop a plan for team training and development.
- Establish a system for managing increased client volume.
- Develop a financial plan for reinvesting in your business growth.

Ready to go deeper? Download the free bonus collection at: www.packagepromotescale.com/bonus

Step 9 – Optimise

As we begin the ninth and final step of our framework, we focus not on reaching an end point but on ensuring that each aspect aligns with who you are and what you stand for. Optimisation isn't just a buzzword; it's the thoughtful calibration of your business to resonate with your deepest values, fulfil the mission you set out to achieve and maximise the value your business delivers to everyone it touches.

You've built a business. Now, let's make sure it's the right business for you. Are you operating in a way that's true to your aspirations? Does your workday reflect your ideal blend of productivity and creativity? Are you able to conduct your business in a way that feels inherently right to you? This is the personal alignment aspect of optimisation, where the business is fine-tuned to fit you like a glove.

It's not just about personal satisfaction; it's also about purpose. Why does your business exist? What mission drives it forward? Optimisation ensures that every strategy, every service and every client interaction reflects this purpose. It's about having a clear vision of what your consultancy stands for and ensuring that every piece of the puzzle contributes meaningfully to that end.

And then, there's value. This isn't just about profits. It's about the value you bring to people's lives and the planet: clients who find solutions, collaborators seeking meaningful partnerships, staff pursuing growth and fulfillment, and a community benefiting from your business's impact. Optimisation means you're consistently refining how your business serves all these stakeholders, ensuring that the value you promise is the value that's felt.

As we look at optimisation through this lens, we find it's about more than efficiency or effectiveness. It's about harmony between your work and your life, your business's actions and its core beliefs and the services you provide and the benefits they bring. It's about making sure your business is a force for good—for you and for all who engage with it.

In this step, we'll explore how to embed this philosophy into the very DNA of your business. We'll look at how to incorporate feedback in a way that furthers your values, revisit goals to ensure they're in service to your mission, streamline operations for efficiency and for greater purpose while fostering a culture where optimisation is a shared responsibility. We'll also discuss how to prepare your business for the future so it remains relevant and resonant, no matter what changes come your way.

This process of optimisation is the path to ensuring that the business you've poured your heart into not only stands the test of time but also remains true to the vision you set out with and delivers value that echoes far beyond the bottom line. This is where your consultancy not only succeeds but also matters. Welcome to the heart of your business's evolution.

***

IMPLEMENTING FEEDBACK LOOPS

Feedback is the compass that guides us towards better service, sharper insights and deeper connections. It's what allows us to align our business with the very heartbeats of those we serve and work with. Implementing feedback loops is about creating a dialogue, a continuous exchange where information flows in, around and back out in the form of improved services and relationships.

Think of feedback as a conversation that involves listening, understanding and then acting. And this conversation starts with being open to what others have to say. Whether it's glowing praise from a client or a constructive suggestion from a team member, each piece of feedback is a thread that can be woven into the fabric of your business to make it stronger and more resilient.

Taking action on feedback demonstrates to your clients and colleagues that you are responsive and proactive. It's one thing to thank someone for their input; it's another to show them the changes you've made because of it. This is where the conversation turns into a visible transformation, reinforcing the trust and respect between you and your stakeholders.

How do we gather this feedback? There are multiple channels, each offering a unique perspective:

- **Standardise With An SOP**

  Create an SOP for how you will collect, analyse and action feedback.

- **Use A Variety Of Methods**

  Use a range of methods to collect feedback such as individual project debriefs with the client and with your team as well as short surveys. Consider also using video tools such as VideoAsk and Loom.

- **Ask Clients Along The Way**

  Client comments and reviews can provide direct insights into how your services are received and where they could be enhanced. Don't wait until the end of the engagement to capture feedback and testimonials.

- **Check In With Collaborators**

  Input from collaborators, employees and partner businesses can offer a behind-the-scenes look at your operations and how they can be improved.

- **Reflect On Your Own Experience**

  Personal introspection and self-reflection are also crucial. Sometimes, the most profound insights come from looking inward and asking yourself hard questions about your satisfaction and alignment with the business.

When you receive positive feedback, it's a golden opportunity to amplify what's working. Transform those affirming comments into testimonials that can bolster your reputation and attract new clients. Success stories not only highlight your achievements but also show potential clients what's possible for them.

But what about when feedback points to areas needing improvement? Here's where the real work begins:

- **Thank The Individual For Their Honesty**

  A simple acknowledgment can go a long way.

- **Evaluate The Feedback**

  Is it a one-off opinion or does it reflect a recurring theme that you need to address?

- **Decide On A Course Of Action**

  What changes can you make to address the issue? This might involve tweaking a process, investing in new tools or even changing the way you communicate.

Feedback shouldn't be a one-way street. Consider ways you can give feedback to the client too about the project, if they're open to it. After you've made changes, close the loop. Go back to those who offered the feedback and tell them how you've used their insights. This not only shows appreciation for their input but also invites them to continue the conversation. Their estimation of you as a person and professional will rise, and they may well become one of your business champions, coming to you with new opportunities that you might not have heard of otherwise.

In implementing these feedback loops, we're aiming for:

- A business that listens and adapts, becoming more in tune with the needs and desires of those it serves.
- Business operations that reflect a deep understanding of both the clients' expectations and your team's capabilities.
- A consultancy practice that doesn't just deliver services but also embodies the values and aspirations you hold dear.

As you optimise your business, recognise that every piece of feedback, every change made, is a step towards a consultancy that's not only a business but a reflection of your best self. It's about building not only a client base but a community around the shared goal of excellence. In this way, feedback becomes more than a tool; it becomes the very pulse of a thriving consultancy.

***

REVISITING YOUR BUSINESS GOALS

Sustaining a prosperous business requires periodic pauses to reassess your goals. The targets you set for yourself when you first started might have been met, or perhaps they've shifted with changes in your industry and personal life. This is the natural course of business evolution, and it calls for a fresh look at your business goals to ensure they still serve you well.

When we say business goals, we're not merely referring to the financial benchmarks or client numbers, although these are important. We're also talking about the alignment of your business operations with your personal values and aspirations. It's about asking yourself whether your business is a true representation of what you stand for and whether it's leading you to where you want to be.

Revisiting your business goals involves:

- **Reflecting On Your Original Business Plan**

  How much of it is still relevant? It's fine if the answer is 'not much.' Businesses grow and adapt, and your plan needs to evolve as well.

- **Evaluating Your Financial Objectives**

  Are you meeting your income targets? Are your profit margins where they need to be? Are you able to pay yourself adequately?

- **Considering Your Lifestyle Goals**

  Think about the satisfaction and impact your business has on your life. Does your business allow you to live the life you envisioned when you started?

- **Determining Your Exit Strategy**

  Do you want to build a business that can run without you to sell?

If you find that your current business goals are no longer serving you, it's time to adjust them. This isn't about starting from scratch but refining what you already have to better fit your business and personal circumstances. Here's how you can approach it:

- **Reaffirm Your 'Big Why'**

  Why did you start this business? Ensure your goals still align with this fundamental reason.

- **Monitor Progress**

  Regularly check how close you are to achieving your goals and identify any areas where you're falling short.

- **Welcome Change**

  If your business or personal circumstances have changed, don't hesitate to modify your goals to reflect this new reality.

Metrics are the signposts that guide us as our business changes, indicating whether we're on the right track. Over time, the metrics you once deemed crucial might no longer reflect your business's current state or future direction. Therefore, it's important to:

- **Review The Relevance Of Your Existing Metrics**

  Do they still measure what matters most to your business? Be mindful of the metrics you choose for indicators of success, sales, profits and growth.

- **Add New Metrics If Necessary**

  As your business grows, new challenges and opportunities arise that might require tracking new metrics.

Streamlining your operations is also a part of revisiting your business goals. It's about making sure that the way you work is as effective and enjoyable as possible. This might involve:

- Identifying processes that can be improved or eliminated. Every task needs to add value to your business or your clients.
- Always considering automation or delegation. Free up your time to focus on strategic thinking or areas of your business that need a personal touch.

However, reassessing your goals doesn't stop at the internal workings of your business. It's also about the impact your business has on the world around you. This involves:

- Assessing the social and environmental impact of your business. Are you contributing positively to your community and the planet?
- Aligning with larger goals. Does your business contribute to the broader objectives related to sustainability, social responsibility and ethical practices?
- Considering how you can integrate principles of environmental stewardship, social responsibility and good

governance into your business and reporting on your contributions.

- Determining whether obtaining certifications or affiliations that recognise your business's positive impact would be beneficial in communicating the difference you make.
- Considering how you can include diversity and inclusion practices in your business to increase economic and social participation through employment, procurement, scholarships etc. Commit to pro bono work, volunteering and sponsorships mindfully so that you can do good work, without burning out or distracting from your business.

Revisiting your business goals is an ongoing process. It's about continuous self-improvement and business development. It is a commitment to ensuring that your consultancy flourishes and remains a source of fulfilment and pride. Take the time to reflect on your goals, measure your progress and adjust your course. Your future self and business will thank you for it.

***

STREAMLINING OPERATIONS

In the life of any consultancy, there comes a time when the way we do things, our operations, needs a second look. It's not about change for the sake of change but is about ensuring that every part of our business is working as smoothly and effectively as possible. This is streamlining operations, a key step in optimisation that can help make your business more agile and your workday less cluttered.

Streamlining begins with a simple yet sometimes challenging question: Is there a better way? Whether it's the process you use to onboard new clients, how you manage your accounts, or even the daily routines you follow, each one needs to help you, not hinder you. Here's a breakdown of what this might look like:

Assessing Current Processes

- Take inventory of the tasks and processes you do regularly.
- Ask yourself and your team if these processes are still serving their intended purpose.

Identifying Bottlenecks

- Look for areas where work seems to get held up regularly.
- Speak to your team and clients about any frustrations they might have with how things are done.

Evaluating Tools And Software

- Check if the tools you're using are the best fit for your needs.
- Consider if there's new software that could do the job better or if you're using your current tools to their full potential.
- Measurement tools such as Seedkit can be useful to track, measure and evaluate your impact.

Once you've identified areas for improvement, it's time to consider how you can make those processes more efficient. Often, the solutions will involve automation or delegation. Automation tools are becoming increasingly sophisticated and can handle a wide range of tasks from scheduling to client communication and billing. Delegation, on the other hand, relies on trusting your team or finding external help to take on tasks that don't require your personal expertise.

The benefits of streamlining operations are numerous:

- **Time Savings**

  Every minute saved is a minute you can spend on higher-value work or enjoying your life outside of work.

- **Cost Efficiency**

  Efficient processes often mean lower costs, as you spend less time on any given task and can avoid the expenses associated with delays or errors.

- **Improved Client Experience**

  Smooth operations result in higher client satisfaction, as they will value the professionalism and ease of working with your consultancy.

- **Employee Satisfaction**

  A streamlined operation can improve job satisfaction for your team, as it allows them to focus on meaningful work without unnecessary administrative burdens.

In streamlining your operations, it's important not to lose sight of the human element. Automation and efficiency must never come at the expense of a personal touch or the quality of your service. The goal is to free up your time and your mind so that you can bring your best self to your clients and your business.

Additionally, as you streamline your operations, keep your broader business goals and values in mind. Every operational decision needs to support these, ensuring that your business remains a true reflection of what you stand for.

Finally, streamlining is not a one-time task but an ongoing practice. It requires you to stay vigilant, keep asking if there's a better way and be willing to make changes when necessary. Constantly improving your business keeps it competitive and helps make it more enjoyable to run.

***

BUILDING A CULTURE OF OPTIMISATION

As a consultant, orchestrating your operations involves more than just managing tasks; it's about cultivating a dynamic environment where collaboration, subcontracting and outsourcing are not only operational necessities but integral parts of a thriving business culture. In this regard, building a culture of optimisation is essential. It ensures that every collaborative effort, every outsourced task, aligns seamlessly with your business goals and values.

- **Fostering Open Communication**

  Keeping the lines of communication open with your collaborators and subcontractors is vital. Regular updates and check-ins ensure everyone is aligned, encouraging a shared approach to continuous improvement.

- **Empowerment In Collaboration**

  Granting a degree of autonomy to your collaborators and subcontractors can lead to new improvements in their areas of expertise. Recognising and appreciating their contributions nurtures a productive and innovative working environment.

- **Continuous Learning**

  Keeping yourself and your team updated with industry trends and encouraging professional development can inject fresh skills and knowledge into your business, enhancing its overall capability.

- **Recognising And Rewarding Innovation**

  Acknowledging and implementing efficient solutions proposed by your team demonstrates that you value their input, encouraging them to continue contributing actively.

- **Iterative Feedback Mechanism**

  A straightforward system for regular input from all parties ensures that everyone's voice is heard and valued. Acting on this feedback fosters a collaborative culture of improvement.

- **Adapting To Change**

  Being adaptable in a dynamic business environment is crucial. Supporting your team through transitions when introducing new processes or tools helps maintain agility and readiness for new challenges.

In this flexible team structure, each collaborator, subcontractor, or outsourced professional adds their own value to your business. It's a network where each member's expertise adds valuable efficiency and effectiveness to your business. Some direct benefits of this approach are:

- Enhanced performance, as insights for improvements often come directly from those handling specific tasks.
- Greater engagement from team members who feel their ideas are valued and see their suggestions come to fruition.
- Increased flexibility and innovation, keeping your business agile and ready to adapt to new challenges and opportunities.

Developing this culture of optimisation goes beyond streamlining processes or adopting the latest tools. It's about creating an ecosystem where every participant, no matter their role's duration, feels empowered to bring their best to the table. It's about blending their expertise with your vision to forge a consultancy that's not only efficient and productive but also resonant with collective success and shared values.

***

FUTUREPROOFING YOUR CONSULTANCY

Futureproofing your consultancy is about preparing today for the successes of tomorrow. It's about staying relevant, resilient and ready to welcome whatever changes the future may bring. In the consulting world, where needs and trends can shift rapidly, futureproofing isn't just a good practice; it's essential for long-term survival and growth.

The first step in futureproofing is staying attuned to your clients' needs. This involves:

- **Regularly Checking In With Clients**

  Make time to understand their changing challenges and expectations.

- **Adapting Services To Meet New Demands**

  Be ready to tweak or overhaul your offerings in response to

client feedback and market shifts.

- **Proactive Learning**

Stay ahead of industry trends that might affect your clients.

Adapting to your clients' evolution is only part of the equation. Keeping an eye on industry trends and innovations is equally important. This means:

- **Attending Industry Conferences And Webinars**

These can be treasure-troves of information about upcoming trends and new methodologies.

- **Networking With Peers**

Conversations with fellow consultants can provide insights into broader market changes and new approaches.

- **Subscribing To Relevant Publications**

Stay updated with the latest industry news and developments.

Building a resilient business model is another key aspect of futureproofing. It involves creating a business capable of withstanding market fluctuations, economic downturns, and global events.

Some strategies to achieve this include:

- **Diversifying Your Client Base**

Avoid over-reliance on a single client or market segment.

- **Having A Financial Cushion**

Maintain a healthy cash reserve to tide you over during lean periods.

- **Using Flexible Business Strategies**

Be ready to pivot your business approach when circumstances change.

In addition to these strategies, exploring new offerings based on market demand and trends is crucial. This might involve:

- Developing new services based on emerging needs or gaps in the market.
- Upskilling through learning new skills or technologies that could expand your service offerings.
- Testing new ideas by experimenting with new concepts on a smaller scale before a full rollout.

While futureproofing your consultancy, it's important to align your actions with your core values and long-term vision. Every step you take needs to be a move toward a more robust business as well as a more personally rewarding experience. This alignment ensures your growth encompasses profitability, satisfaction, and personal achievement.

Futureproofing your consultancy also means being mindful of your impact on the community and the environment. This involves:

- Adopting environmentally friendly practices in your operations.
- Getting involved in community initiatives or volunteering your services to nonprofits.

Futureproofing your consultancy is about being prepared, adaptable, and aligned with your core values. It's about creating a business that thrives in the face of change.

***

OTHER CONSIDERATIONS

In rounding out our strategy for optimising your consultancy, it's important to consider several additional facets that contribute to a well-rounded, responsible and impactful business. While the core focus is often on profitability and efficiency, integrating broader societal and environmental considerations can enrich your consultancy's role in the community and the world.

- **Sustainable Business Practices**

  Sustainable practices are key. This goes beyond being eco-friendly to ensuring your entire business operation minimises its environmental footprint. Consider using digital rather than physical resources to reduce waste, implementing energy-saving practices in your office and choosing suppliers and collaborators who also adhere to sustainable practices.

- **Community Engagement**

  Actively engaging with your community is vital. Your expertise can powerfully support local programs and nonprofits. Consider offering pro bono services, volunteering for community projects or local business mentoring and participating in or sponsoring local events.

- **Ethical Business Operations**

  At the core of a reputable consultancy are its ethical business operations. Maintain high standards in your dealings to ensure long-term success and respect. This means conducting business transparently and fairly, upholding integrity in all decisions and ensuring confidentiality and trust are never compromised.

- **Personal and Professional Development**

  Personal and professional growth is crucial. As a consultant, your development and that of your collaborators directly ties to business success. Stay updated with industry changes, invest in ongoing education and skill development and encourage and support your collaborators' professional growth.

- **Diversity and Inclusion**

  Diversity and inclusion need to be a priority in your business model. Create an environment where diverse perspectives are valued. Be conscious of diversity in your collaborations and foster an inclusive approach in your professional interactions.

- **Supporting Local Businesses**

  Strengthen your community's economy by supporting local businesses. This can involve choosing local suppliers for your business needs and collaborating with other local professionals or small businesses.

- **Mindfulness and Wellbeing**

  Focusing on mindfulness and wellbeing can significantly impact your work environment and effectiveness. Incorporate practices that support mental and physical wellbeing and promote a balanced approach to work among your collaborators.

Integrating these considerations into your consultancy does more than just build a successful business; it crafts an entity that positively affects society, supports the local community, and operates on principles of sustainability and ethics. This comprehensive approach transforms your consultancy into a source of income, a positive influence, and a model of responsible business practices.

***

CONCLUSION

As we conclude this step and our discussion of the Package Promote Scale Framework, let's take a moment to reflect on the progress we've made and the opportunities that lie ahead. This final step, focusing on optimisation, is more than just a set of strategies and tasks; it's the embodiment of a mindset, one that sees continuous improvement as a vital component of success.

Throughout this book, we've explored various facets of optimising your consultancy. From streamlining operations to adapting to changes in the market and your personal life, the goal has been to create a consultancy that doesn't just exist in the present but is prepared for the future. It's about building a business that aligns with your values, meets your clients' needs and contributes positively to the broader community.

The key takeaways from our exploration include:

- **The Importance Of Staying Attuned To Your Clients' Changing Needs And Preferences**

  As their requirements change, your services need to adapt accordingly.

- **Keeping An Eye On Industry Trends And Innovations**

  This proactive approach ensures that your consultancy remains relevant and competitive.

- **The Significance Of Building A Resilient Business Model**

  A consultancy that can withstand market fluctuations and external shocks is one that is built for longevity.

- **Exploring New Offerings Based On Market Demands**

  Diversifying your services can open new opportunities and revenue streams.

The process of optimisation is never truly complete. It requires you to remain flexible, open-minded, and committed to growth to stay ahead of the game.

As you move forward, keep in mind the guiding principles that have underpinned this step with the Package Promote Scale Framework:

- Understand yourself and your motivations, challenge limiting beliefs and align your business with your personal aspirations.
- Analyse your market continuously, position yourself strategically to stand out and find opportunities in untapped areas.
- Craft your message with clarity and authenticity, ensuring it resonates with your audience and reflects your unique voice.

- Build and nurture your network, engage with your audience and foster a community around your brand.
- Embrace continuous learning and growth, adapt your strategies to align with market dynamics and stay updated.
- Maintain authentic communication and branding, ensuring every interaction is consistent and reflects your brand's values.
- Implement a purpose-driven strategy, align every action with your business's overarching purpose and measure your progress.

As an independent consultant, you have an opportunity to shape your business in a way that exhibits your personal values and professional ambitions. The path to optimisation goes beyond enhancing business processes and involves creating a consultancy that is a true representation of who you are and what you believe in.

In closing, your consultancy is more than just a business; it reflects your values and aspirations. The steps you take to optimise it today will lay the foundation for its success tomorrow and for years to come. So, embrace continuous improvement, stay true to your values and look forward to a future filled with possibilities and achievements.

***

CASE STUDY

Maz, a leadership development consultant, had successfully streamlined her operations and built a thriving business. However, as her consultancy grew, she realised that standing still was not an option. Maz understood that continuous optimisation was the key to staying relevant and delivering exceptional value to her clients.

One of the challenges Maz faced was keeping abreast of the changes within her own field. With new theories, tools and best practices emerging constantly, Maz knew she needed a structured approach to stay informed and incorporate the newest approaches and tools into her work.

Another challenge was ensuring that her services remained perfectly aligned with her clients' changing needs. As the social enterprises she worked with grew and faced new challenges, Maz wanted her offerings to keep up by providing the most relevant and effective support.

To address these challenges, Maz implemented a continuous optimisation approach. First, she established a robust feedback loop to gather insights from her clients, team and industry network. She created a regular schedule of check-ins, surveys and follow-up calls to collect valuable input on her services, processes, and overall client satisfaction.

Maz also set aside dedicated time each month for what she called her 'optimisation day'. On these days, she analysed the feedback she had gathered, reviewed industry trends and research and brainstormed ideas for enhancing her offerings. She would then prioritise the most promising ideas and create action plans for implementation.

One of the key insights Maz gained through this process was the growing demand for virtual leadership development programs, particularly among clients with teams spread across several locations. In response, Maz invested in learning about the best practices for online facilitation and adapted her signature workshops into engaging virtual formats. Proactively addressing this shift in client needs allowed Maz to expand her reach and deliver even greater impact. She also explored a range of online technologies and tools through which she could deliver a range of off-the-shelf trainings and live calls that facilitated collaboration over the internet.

Another area of optimisation that Maz focused on was her own professional development. She recognised that investing in her skills and knowledge was crucial to staying at the forefront of her field. Maz committed to attending at least one industry conference per year and enrolled in online courses to deepen her expertise in emerging areas of leadership development. She also joined a mastermind group of fellow consultants, creating a space for peer learning and accountability.

Maz also looked for opportunities to optimise her business model. After careful analysis of her financial data and client feedback, she identified a set of her most impactful and in-demand services. Focusing her efforts on these 'signature offerings' and streamlining her portfolio allowed Maz to increase her efficiency, profitability, and overall client satisfaction.

Maz's commitment to continuous optimisation had a profound effect on her business. Her clients raved about the ever-increasing value and relevance of her services, leading to higher engagement, retention and referral rates. Maz's team was energised by a culture of growth and opportunity, feeling empowered to offer their own ideas for improvement.

For Maz, the optimisation experience was not only professionally rewarding but also personally fulfilling. Remaining open to change allowed her to continue doing the work she loved while making a meaningful difference in the lives of her clients.

***

Lessons Learned

Here are the key takeaways from Maz's path to personal growth:

- **Establish Feedback Loops**

  Regularly gather input from clients, team members and industry peers to stay attuned to changing needs and opportunities for improvement.

- **Dedicate Time For Optimisation**

  Set aside focused time to analyse feedback, review industry

trends and brainstorm ideas for enhancing your offerings.

- **Stay Agile And Adaptable**

  Be willing to pivot and adjust your services in response to changing client needs and market dynamics.

- **Invest In Your Own Development**

  Continuously upgrade your skills and knowledge to stay at the forefront of your field.

- **Optimise Your Business Model**

  Regularly review your portfolio and financial data to identify opportunities for streamlining and focusing on your most impactful offerings.

- **Cultivate A Culture Of Continuous Improvement**

  Empower your team to contribute ideas and insights for optimisation, fostering a shared commitment to growth and excellence.

In adopting these lessons and making continuous optimisation a core part of your business strategy, you will help keep your business relevant, deliver exceptional value to your clients and find greater fulfilment in your work.

***

ACTION STEPS

Optimising your consulting business is an ongoing process that requires continuous improvement and adaptation. Follow these action steps to ensure your business remains efficient, effective and aligned with your goals:

- Collect feedback from clients and team members and make improvements.
- Establish regular intervals for reviewing and updating your business goals.
- Develop KPIs for each area of your business.
- Review your business metrics regularly.

- Implement a system for testing and refining new ideas or processes.
- Establish a process for streamlining and automating repetitive tasks.
- Review work quality as you scale and adjust.
- Review your business model periodically and adapt as needed.
- Implement a process for evaluating and optimising client satisfaction.
- Commit to continual improvement of your work environment and culture.

Ready to go deeper? Download the free bonus collection at: www.packagepromotescale.com/bonus

Conclusion & Next Steps

We've reached the end of our discussion on how to build a more efficient, less stressful, and profitable consulting business. Whilst we're wrapping up this book, your own journey is just beginning—or at the very least taking an important turn.

When we first opened this dialogue, we laid out the common challenges faced by small business consultants, issues that may resonate with your own experiences. These challenges, such as overwork, inconsistent income and operational inefficiencies, are not only common but can be downright debilitating. And yet the situation is not all doom and gloom. In fact, many consultants, just like you, have worked their way through these challenges and are now thriving. How? The answer lies in a structured, systematic approach to business operations, marketing and scalability, which we've thoroughly discussed in this book.

The Package Promote Scale Framework is designed to be your compass, guiding you through the challenges that lie ahead in your consulting business. Following this 3-phase, 9-step approach not only tackles problems as they arise, but also pre-emptively solves issues before they grow into major obstacles. Whether you're just starting out or are well-established, this book offers a path forward for a more organised, less stressful and more profitable business.

In the Package phase, we explored the importance of streamlining services, testing your packages and refining them based on market feedback (Steps 1, 2 and 3). In the Promote phase, we defined an effective marketing approach by attracting the right clients, launching your offerings and managing your sales pipeline (Steps 4, 5 and 6). Finally, in the Scale phase, we explored how to create sustainable business growth through systems, teamwork and optimisation (Steps 7, 8 and 9).

As you turn the final pages of this book, it's crucial to recognise that success doesn't happen overnight. However, armed with the right framework, you are setting yourself up for a journey filled with less stress, more joy, and increased revenue.

***

TAKING ACTION: YOUR NEXT STEPS

Having the knowledge is one thing, but implementing it is what sets apart a thriving business from a stagnant one. As you're reading this book, you already have a powerful blueprint for success in your hands. The question now is: What will you do with it?

1. **Start With Self-Assessment**

   Before commencing any of the steps, take a hard look at where your business stands today. What's working? What isn't working? This introspective exercise will help you tailor the Package Promote Scale Framework to your business environment.

2. **Create A Timeline**

   Success isn't an overnight endeavour. Set realistic timeframes for when you want to complete each of the nine steps.

3. **Involve Your Team**

   If you have staff or collaborators, make sure they're on the same page. Whether it's getting feedback on service packages or input on marketing strategies, collective brainpower often leads to more effective solutions.

4. Monitor, Measure, Adapt

No plan survives first contact with the market. Be ready to adapt your strategies based on real-world feedback and performance metrics. Use KPIs to quantify your success at each step.

5. Celebrate The Wins, Learn From The Losses

Every success, no matter how small, is proof that you're moving in the right direction. Equally, every failure is a lesson in disguise. Celebrate both. They are your stepping stones to greater success.

6. Seek Help When Needed

No one knows everything. If you find yourself stuck at any point, don't hesitate to consult experts, whether they are in the field of marketing, operational efficiency or any other area you're less familiar with.

7. Stay Updated

The business landscape is always changing. New tools, technologies and market conditions can affect your consultancy. Keep learning and adapt to stay ahead of the curve.

8. Repeat The Cycle

Once you've gone through all nine steps, don't think of it as the end. Businesses change over time and your strategies need to evolve as well. Return to the Package Promote Scale Framework periodically to reassess and readjust your plans.

You now have a plan with clear steps. It's up to you to act on it. Building a profitable, low-stress business takes effort, planning, and a dash of courage. Take the first step today. You'll be glad you did.

***

REFLECTING ON YOUR ACCOMPLISHMENTS

By this point, you haven't just read a book; you've engaged with a comprehensive framework for rethinking, revitalising and possibly even reinventing your consulting business. As we near the end of our guide, it's crucial to pause and reflect.

1. **Acknowledge The Progress**

   If you've implemented even a fraction of what has been discussed, you've made progress. It might be subtle or seismic, but either way, it deserves acknowledgment. Take a moment to pat yourself on the back; running a business is no small feat and every step forward is a victory.

2. **The Ongoing Journey Of Improvement**

   Even as you advance through the Package Promote Scale Framework, keep in mind that no business can ever claim to have 'arrived'. There's always room for improvement, innovation and growth.

3. **Personal Growth**

   We've emphasised throughout this book that it's not just about business transformation but also about personal growth. Being a business owner presents distinct challenges that push you to develop new skills, cultivate emotional resilience, and deepen your self-awareness.

4. **Community Impact**

   Your business doesn't operate in a vacuum. As you grow, you're better positioned to contribute positively to your community— whether it's by creating jobs, solving pressing problems or being a model of ethical entrepreneurship.

5. **Visualise The Future**

   What does success look like for you and your business five years from now? Ten years? Use the plans and strategies you've laid out as the stepping stones to that envisioned future.

6. **Legacy Thinking**

   Consider what you want your lasting impact to be. Your business is a powerful platform for creating a legacy that goes beyond financial success. What values, impacts or changes do you want to leave behind?

7. **The Importance Of Balance**

   As you take your next steps in your business and in life, remember that life isn't all about work and revenue. Make time for your health, family and wellbeing. A balanced life contributes to a sustainable and fulfilling business venture.

***

Keep these reflections in mind daily. They will anchor you when things get rough and remind you why you chose this challenging yet incredibly rewarding path in life in the first place.

Build that thriving consultancy you have always dreamed of. You've got this!

Your Feedback Matters

HELP US GROW AND IMPROVE

We invite you to share your thoughts on this book and how it has impacted you and your consulting business. Your insights will help us with future editions and create resources that empower consultants like you.

How to Provide Feedback

- Email: Send your questions, ideas or suggestions to us at: feedback@packagepromotescale.com
- Social media: Use the hashtag #PackagePromoteScale to share your 'aha' moments, success stories or how you've applied the book's principles.

How Your Feedback Helps

Your feedback fuels growth for the entire consulting community. Here's how it makes a difference:

- **Evolving The Book**

  We'll use your input to refine the Package Promote Scale Framework, ensuring it remains at the cutting edge.

- **Creating Resources**

  We'll dive deeper into common challenges and create targeted blog posts, webinars or worksheets to address them.

- **Amplifying Your Voice**

  With your permission, we'll showcase your success stories and insights via our newsletter, social media or website to educate and motivate fellow consultants.

- **Fostering Community**

  Sharing your thoughts contributes to a supportive community of consultants, sparking conversations, collaborations, and breakthroughs.

Your feedback supports the continuous improvement of this book and the entire ecosystem of consultants building thriving businesses.

Join the conversation. Your voice matters! Thank you for being part of our journey. Together, we can redefine what's possible in consulting.

Visit us at www.packagepromotescale.com to learn more!